AL KHOZAMA

Kanakaraj Balasubramanyam

Translated by
Aswini Kumar

ZERO DEGREE PUBLISHING

AL KHOZAMA © Kanakaraj Balasubramanyam
AL KHOZAMA © Translated from Tamil by Aswini Kumar
First Edition by Zero Degree Publishing: July 2024

ISBN: 978-93-95233-26-2
ZDP Title: 68

ZERO DEGREE PUBLISHING
No.55(7), R Block, 6th Avenue,
Anna Nagar,
Chennai - 600 040

Website: www.zerodegreepublishing.com-
E Mail id: zerodegreepublishing@gmail.com
Phone : 89250 61999

Cover Design & Typeset: Vijayan, Creative Studio
Printed in India

AL KHOZAMA

Every moment happens twice: inside and outside,
and they are different histories.

- Zadie Smith

1

As he was wondering, "Why did I have that dream now when no one from our *faqat* (clan) has been killed recently?", a large desert lizard, known locally as the *dabb*, caught his eye as it quietly slithered into an underground burrow.

Shuja ibn Saqr ibn Mohammed ibn Hamad ibn Ahmed al-Zoubi al-Sodari stared unblinkingly at the spot where the *dabb* had hid itself, making mental plans to catch it when it resurfaced. As memories of the effort it had taken to catch one of them a few years back and the delicious taste of its meat flooded back, a different thought struck him: would he succeed in siring a male child if he ate *dabb* meat every day? This query rose from his throat and spread upwards to his brain, much to his delight. He stood up and looked around him at the immense expanse of the desert, the sand dunes in the distance, stunted trees and shrubs spread around - and enveloping them all a vast, empty silence.

Shuja's thoughts went back to when he had last visited this spot.

It would have been six to seven years now. It was before the wedding. There - that's the place where the *khozama* flowers had bloomed and were dancing in the wind. That was indeed a very special moment. That was the time when my friend Saeed and I stayed here for two whole days. We had stayed awake through the night, looking out at the rain from inside our tent.

It was amusing when he now thought back about the reason why he had come to this spot all those years ago.

That was the day my sister Maha had got married. It was my wish that she marry my second *a'ammi*'s (paternal uncle's) son whereas my father decided to give her in marriage to his fifth brother's son. Unable to tolerate it, I had run off to this spot instead of attending the wedding ceremony.

And here I am today with Maha's husband at the very same spot!

When winter is done and the first rains fall, I need to come back here again to enjoy the scent of the *khozama* flowers.

But what's the use of appreciating all that? *Ya Allah*! Why has the Almighty, the most merciful, not been benevolent enough to grant me a son? Amongst us Bedouins, inability to sire a male child is a huge loss of face. All I ask of the Almighty is one son....just one male child....to uphold the pride of our al-Zoubi clan.

Despite having two wives, not one son has resulted. I lack the wherewithal to take another wife. That would require at least a hundred thousand riyals. I am still paying back the previous bank loans availed to finance my two earlier marriages. In the circumstances, how can I even consider a third one? The *meher* to the new bride alone would set me back by over fifty thousand riyals. On top of that add the expenses towards another house, furniture, fixtures.....Ya Allah! And my monthly salary is only eight thousand riyals.

If I were to go to Misr (Egypt), the Maghreb (Morocco/Algeria/Tunisia), Al-Hind (India) or Pakistan to marry a girl from any of these countries, my own brothers would look down upon me with contempt. It would be a matter of shame if I were to marry a non-Bedouin girl.

What was that fragrance? Does *khozama* bloom even during winter?

Shuja turned. His brother-in-law Mohammed ibn Saud al-Sodari was coming towards him holding some roots of the *samar* tree in his hands.

Shuja ran towards Mohammed saying, "*Mashallah, mashallah*". He took the *samar* roots from Mohammed and, holding them up to his nose, inhaled the aroma deeply.

"*Al Hamdullillah*! What a lovely fragrance when we are about to depart from this place. Now listen to this," said Shuja ibn Saqr al-Zoubi al-Sodari, and recited a poem that he had composed on the spot:

Our treasure
That
Tames the Wild Sands,
I bloom
And every time
I near you
I am reinvigorated.

You are created in warmth
Whilst ensconced in
Every shred of our hearts.
Yet again
You move towards us
Occasionally stretching
The rims of the clouds
To deposit droplets down upon us.

You are the glitter
In the treasury
That is our desert.

You are the
Beauteous plumage
That gladdened the hearts of our
Ancestors.
You are our
Bounteous Treasure.....

When Shuja completed his recitation, Mohammed ibn Saud al-Sodari exclaimed appreciatively, *"Vunnar min sababa"* (excellent) as he climbed into the jeep. He then laughingly commented, "Your winters are never complete without logs from the *samar* trees, right?"

The jeep carrying the stack of *samar* logs started towards the city.

The desert soil surrounded by mountain ranges would turn arable with the occasional rainfall. At other times, at best, it would support the growth of small plants and creepers. The *samar* which grows in such an environment would exude a pleasant fragrance when burned. Not just that, it would also smoulder slowly releasing smoke without flames. The fragrant smoke emitted by it would gladden the souls of everyone around it.

Most bedouins preferred the heat generated by burning the *samar* wood during winters. Even if they owned electric heaters, they would rather have their houses heated by these trees from the desert.

The jeep crisscrossed the sand dunes. As both of them kept chatting and fiddling with their phones checking for a signal, they reached a particular spot which made them look at each other and laugh.

Four years ago, on a wintry night, they had come to camp at this place called Nuebath and pitched a tent here. They were both well aware of the legend that this area was inhabited by *jinns* which made spending the night in the desert during winters a dangerous proposition. As neither of them believed in the existence of *jinns* they had come here to camp just to prove their friends wrong. A story also made its rounds among the younger bedouins that whenever one of their *ibn a'ammi* (paternal cousin) came to this spot to recite his poems, hordes of cats would suddenly appear. Surely they were *jinns*, in their opinion. Otherwise, how else do you explain cats that only reside in cities turning out in droves in the middle of the desert? Both of them strongly disagreed with the bedouins' belief that the poet was possessed by a *jinn* and it was this spirit which was behind the verses produced by the man. It was to shatter this belief that they had come here then, disregarding the cold weather, and spent the night roaming the area spinning their poetry and joking. It was the memory of that night which provoked their laughter now.

In the midst of that laughter, Shuja ibn Saqr was once again reminded of last night's dream.

Why did that *Hindi* (Indian) boy from Al-Majeed garage appear in my dream? I must have seen him around only once or twice at that place, so what caused him to appear in my dream? He also said something....what was it?

Struggling to recall the dream, Shuja turned to his cousin and asked, "Ya Mohammed, you said something this morning....didn't you?"

"Did I? What about? I don't remember...."

"You said you met someone at Tamra last week....?"

"Oh, that? Some old man...I don't think he's from our *faqat*....but he was using old colloquial Arabic slang just like our elders do. Why do you ask about him now?" Mohammed saw the desert in Shuja's eyes.

"I had a dream last night. In it, a *Hindi* boy appeared and asked me, 'Has it been ten years now since your *ibn a'ammi* (nephew) was killed?'" Shuja's eyes were fixated on the sand dunes opposite.

"You people will never learn," said Mohammed in a harsh tone, masking the elation in his heart.

The reason for the argument was the dream that had appeared to Shuja the previous night. In that dream, an Indian, a young man named Rajendran from South India, had appeared dressed in a *thobe* (Arabic robe) and berated Shuja, "You are a shameless *bedu*.... Instead of seeking revenge for the killing of your father's younger brother, you are enjoying a cushy life...." That provocation had kindled a raging fire within Shuja's innards and was heating up his brain as he traversed the desert. Vendetta was very common among the bedouins within Arab society, particularly among the al-Sodari tribe and especially among the al-Zoubi clan. In Shuja's dream, Rajendran was appearing in a TV interview and was speaking fluent Arabic while describing the bedouin way of life.

"Our tribe has historically inhabited the desert regions of Arabia even before the advent of Islam. Our society followed several unwritten rules such as complete trust, generosity, unbounded courtesy, self-respect and the willingness to sacrifice our life in order to protect our clan and its honour. We would go to any extent to uphold these principles. Of the three subsections - Bedouins, *Hadari* and Black Arabs - we, the **Bedouins** are at the very top of the hierarchy. It is true that Islam does not recognise such differentiations....but this is how it is. One more important point: we do not encourage mixing of bloodlines and we would not enter into marriage alliances with any other subsect. We strongly believe in maintaining the purity of our bloodline. Once a nomadic race, travelling around with our camels throughout the Arabian peninsula, most of us have now, like the *Hadari*, settled down at fixed abodes and turned into cultivators. The history of our race, which used to forever shift like the sand dunes in the desert wind, is a very ancient one. Deep loyalties and sworn enmities are both ingrained in our psyche. We would lend a helping hand to even our enemies if they were ever in trouble. We would consider it our duty to protect those who came to us seeking refuge at the cost of our own lives. Our credo is: an eye for an eye but abiding loyalty in return for friendship. However, the bedouins of the modern day have changed and the proof of this is right here in front of you, this man: Shuja ibn Saqr al-Zoubi al-Sodari. Just look at him....sleeping soundly, unconcerned that his father's own sibling had been killed. Let the camera zoom in on his face....let the whole world watch him and scorn him....." This was the moment when Shuja had woken up with a start. He was fuming at Rajendran who had appeared in his dream. The details of the nightmare which he had forgotten suddenly became clear to him as he entered the desert, and shook him up badly.

Talking to himself, Shuja mumbled, "While I cannot think of anyone who has been killed recently from our clan, I am also unable to explain this dream...."

"Did you forget we lost Naif last month? I do not know when you people are ever going to stop," said Mohammed in a bitter warning tone.

This silenced Shuja for a while. He then looked at Mohammed and commented sadly, "When I think back how we failed to extricate him from punishment by paying *diya*, I don't feel like carrying on living, *Abu* Hasan...."

Hasan is Mohammed's son. In Arab society males are often addressed respectfully by mentioning their son's name and adding the appellation '*abu*' or "father of" before it. This is how Shuja addressed his sister's husband, Mohammed. While calling him by this title, it gave him immense pain to be still addressed by his father's name. If a man did not have a male child, it was usual to call him employing his father's name. With the idea that he would name his future son after his father, everybody addressed him as "Abu Saqr", and that plunged him into deeper distress.

Ya Allah...one son.... just one male child....

Mohammed's words, instead of entering Abu Saqr's ears, were dissipating in the air. Naif ibn Ahmed al-Zoubi al-Sodari, one of their tribesmen, had recently killed a person belonging to the al-Mulaqim clan. He had been arrested, tried and sentenced to death by beheading. The al-Mulaqims had gone to the police instead of seeking vengeance and killing a person from the Al-Zoubi clan in retaliation. Naif had been arrested within just three days and brought before a court. His guilt had been established and the death sentence pronounced. By citing the pathetic condition of Naif's family, the affected family was somehow convinced by some of the al-Zoubis to accept *diya*, the financial compensation paid to the heirs of a victim. But they had been unable to pay the amount of the *diya* that was demanded. It was then widely rumoured that the al-Mulaqims had deliberately demanded an unconscionably high *diya* and, by that means, not only did they manage to settle their score but also exposed the al-Zoubi's powerlessness to the whole country. This had created a strong sense of anger and sorrow among the al-Zoubis. Shuja ibn Saqr was one such person. He was waiting for the right opportunity to wreak his vengeance upon the al-Mulaqims and had reached the first step towards that impulse.

"Hey listen…when my grandfather's youngest brother was killed, the murderer went underground. It was rumoured that he had run off to Iraq. My father then went to Iraq looking for him….I was just a kid then…." human instincts roiled within Shuja's heart and a red mist descended upon his brain.

"*Ya rajhil,"* (Oh man) when will your feud with the al-Mulaqims come to an end?" asked Mohammed wishing to further infuriate Shuja by reminding him of the Naif episode.

"How can it end? How do you expect a disagreement that has been in existence from pre-Islamic times to end suddenly now? It's a feud going back over two thousand years…." Shuja's veins throbbed with suppressed fury.

“They are more powerful than us both in wealth and position…. however much you try, you simply can’t beat them….” Mohammed went on provoking Shuja.

“Thieving bastards….their clan has survived all these years by means of thieving….”

“Hahaha…you are forgetting that they’re also our fraternal clan….” laughed Mohammed loudly.

“Who’ll accept them as part of our fraternity? Our ancestors had always wanted to eliminate them totally ….but apparently, it was our family that forbade it. Do you know something, Abu Hasan? You know our next of kin, the al-Khamarims? Before embracing Islam, they used to worship their tribal deity - a tree - and leave offerings such as wheat, rice and fruits to it. It is said that these thieving dogs, the al-Mulaqims, would then appear, steal those offerings and run off with them….” as he kept speaking, he was mentally calculating the route to Tamra where he could meet with the newly-arrived elder.

“Hahaha…yes, I’ve heard those stories also….but didn’t they force the Turkish army to retreat from Najd?”

“Shut up….did you think they fought with the Turks? It was our clan who defeated them and sent them packing….all the al-Mulaqims did was steal guns, foodstuff and clothes from the Turkish army and slink away like the cowardly crooks that they are ....”

“Doesn’t that also count as a tactic of war, eh?”

“I spit on such cowardly tactics….”

“Whatever you say….there’s still no one to match them in influence or money power….”

“However influential they may be, we’ll still find a way to teach them a lesson….” said Shuja furiously. By now he had finally figured out a way to meet with the elder who had recently arrived in Tamra. Blood lust continued to surge in his veins.

As Mohammed muttered, “When will you ever give up all this violence and start following the true teachings of Islam…..?”

Shuja was gazing silently at the empty desert.

2

Rajendran stood up and tried the door. It appeared to be locked from the outside. His legs twitched as though wanting to kick it down.

He stood staring at the door for a while. Feeling as though he had been cast into a dark cell, he slumped down in dejection. That is when he remembered that dream.

Rajendran paused in his headlong run across the desert in bewilderment. How many more miles did he have to cover? He hadn't even crossed Saudi Arabia yet. While he stood there thinking it had been three nights and four days since he started running from Al Sulayyil, the small town where he was employed, the Arab appeared - the bedouin Arab: Shuja ibn Saqr al-Zoubi al-Sodari!

Rajendran was totally taken aback to hear the Arab speak to him in Tamil in the dream. He was surprised that Shuja ibn Saqr, who had never been to India, and especially to South India, could speak that language so fluently. He wondered if his cousin and the proprietor of the garage, Sundar, had taught him conversational Tamil. He however recalled that during his occasional visits to the garage Shuja would talk to Sundar only in Arabic. Then it came to him why Shuja had appeared in his dream: he had been accused of stealing a bag from Shuja's car while it was in their garage.

Looking at a mirror in the wall, Rajendran spoke to himself:

Why would I steal the bag from that Arab's car? I know very well he is a *bedu*. He didn't believe my protestations. But, my cousin, Sundar should have known better. Why would I steal that *bedu*'s property? I am sure Sundar himself must have stolen that bag and then blamed me for it. Yes, I'm sure that, because the Arab was not paying his bill for the last repairs to his car on time, Sundar must have done it himself. When I see that Arab the next time, I'll tell him what I suspect.

When Shuja ibn Saqr al-Zoubi al-Sodari appeared in Rajendran's dream, Rajendran was seated on a sand dune in the desert completely exhausted. The sun was setting but the heat was still radiating like an oven. The western sky was awash in red. As he sat there appreciating the wind spreading its music and rearranging the desert sands, Rajendran watched in shock as a Land Cruiser came barreling towards him at high speed. When it neared him, he recognised the driver as the bedouin Arab, Shuja ibn Saqr al-Zoubi al-Sodari who would occasionally patronise the garage he worked in. Shuja addressed him in Tamil:

"Where are you off to - Riyadh or Jeddah?"

After silently staring at him for a short while, Rajendran replied, "Back home."

"Come along. I'll drop you off at Riyadh," said Shuja, as he practically forced Rajendran into his vehicle and set off.

"What's in the bag?" he asked, looking at Rajendran.

"Clothes, what else?" replied Rajendran lightly and turned to look outside the window.

"You haven't bought chocolates or perfumes for your folk back home?"

Rajendran turned towards him, shook his head negatively, and said, "I've no money for all that stuff. My *mudir* (owner), my own cousin, hasn't paid me regularly for the past two years. He claims that I still owe him for expenses, like visa charges, insurance premium etc. that he incurred to bring me over here in the first place. In addition, he makes me work like a dog…from eight in the morning till midnight. Yes, he does feed me, but is that sufficient? Do you know how my parents used to pamper me? They sent me to this country trusting this fellow's words. Do you know what he has told my parents? He's told them I have paid back all his expenses and have begun to earn my own money now. I am supposed to be splurging it all here instead of sending some of it back home to them. And they believe his nonsense as gospel and are unwilling to listen to any of my explanations. I accept I was a wastrel back home. Thinking I'd acquire some sense if I went abroad, my mother pawned the only gold chain she owned and financed my trip. That's when I made up my mind that I'd behave responsibly from now on…since my arrival in Saudi till date I've not spent a single riyal on nonessentials or luxuries of any kind. You may find it hard to believe, but for the last two years I have not even had a sip of Pepsi. Did you know how he thrashed me one day on the suspicion that I was doing outside work and taking payment for it? I am a twenty-year old man, not a child. Since I was already under suspicion, I began to moonlight in the hope of saving some money and running off to Riyadh. My passport is stuck with my *kafeel* (local sponsor) and he certainly wouldn't release it if I went and asked him for it to go back home. This year I'll have to cough up at least another ten thousand riyals towards renewal of my visa and *iqama* (residence permit) as well as my travel expenses. How am I going to raise such a sum? All I've is two thousand riyals. That's why I'm planning to go to Riyadh, get myself arrested and, under the guise of amnesty for undocumented workers, make my way back to India…."

"Are you really only twenty years old? You must be joking! But that aside, why do you want to go to India?"

Rajendran laughed and replied, "If not India, where else would I go, boss?"

"Aren't you a Sudani? Why would you go to India?"

Rajendran again laughed and asked, "Do I look like a Sudani to you?" He then leant out of the window and looked at himself in the side mirror and was stunned at what he saw!

What's this? I look like a fifty year old man....and that too a Sudani! Oh my God! What's happening? Have I suddenly aged? Have I been abroad for such a long time then? Have I grown old without even realising it myself?

He turned to look back. He was on a dune...in the midst of the vast desert....that bedu, Shuja....where is he? Wasn't I travelling in his vehicle? My bag....where's it?

He ran like a man possessed....checked every sand dune around.... the bag was nowhere in sight.

The bag contained some twenty-five thousand riyals....My God! That was nearly five hundred thousand Indian rupees. Oh God....

Surely the *bedu* must have taken it....I should have been on my guard when he enquired about the contents of my bag....

There....there's the jeep again....it must be him! Come on, come nearer, you motherfucker....

"Hello *maplai* (literally son-in-law)....were you getting ready to return home?"

What's this? It was Raghu *mama* (maternal uncle) in the landcruiser! Where was he - the Arab - who had stolen my money? And how did Raghu *mama* land up in Saudi Arabia? Everything is so confusing....

"Listen *maplai*....your father is defaulting on his interest payments. This five hundred thousand would just about cover a year's interest. Please make sure the principal is repaid as early as possible....I've arranged for my daughter's wedding and I need the money urgently ...."

"Please give it back *mama*....it's not right....this money is meant for construction of our house....if you don't give it back, I'll not be responsible for my actions.....I swear I'll kill you....I won't even care that you're my uncle....Motherfucker! Give me my money back...."

Rajendran woke up with a start.

What sort of dream was this? It was incomprehensible....

The door remained shut ...."*Anna* (elder brother), Sundar *anna*, please open the door....I need to go to the bathroom...."

3

Shuja ibn Saqr al-Zoubi al-Sodari's great-great-grandfather, Ahmed ibn Rashid ibn Saqr ibn Shuja ibn Marri ibn Bandar ibn Shuja ibn Marri al-Zoubi al-Sodari herded his camels into their enclosure. The sun's rays fell on the animals' heads as they milled about in the pen.

Ahmed ibn Rashid was returning after offering the afternoon's *asr* prayers. Not content with castigating his brother, Abdullah ibn Rashid al-Sodari for not attending the prayers, he also berated his fellow bedouins, "Uncivilised barbarians....savages who do not realise the power of prayers....may Allah show you the right path...." as he prepared to milk the camels.

He needed to finish milking before night fell. By the time he and his five sons finished their milking, it would be time for the *adhan* call for the *maghrib* prayers. His second son, Saeed, had gone into town. Saeed was the most energetic of all his sons and was capable of milking six camels in double quick time. He also prayed five times a day without fail.

"The grandchildren need to be admitted into the *madrasa*....they need to learn the proper teachings of Islam....*insha'allah*...." Ahmed muttered to himself as he concentrated on his task.

His third son, Minah was humming a bedouin song softly to himself. Minah's abiding wish was to attend the Okaz poetry festival and present one of his poems at the conclave. Once a year poets from all over Arabia participated in a competition held at Okaz and presented their best compositions. The standard and quality of the recitations was so high that they sometimes left even the judges stunned. The al-Sodari bedouins were also in the habit of participating in the competition. Every subsect of the Sodari tribe boasted of talented poets. They would select one among their lot to represent the whole tribe at the Okaz event. Minah's long-standing ambition was to participate in the competition at least once in his lifetime. He had even composed a special poem for the occasion. Unfortunately, his father was as dead set against the poetry competition as he was against camel racing. Any time either topic came up at home, he would blow his top. He was of the opinion that both these activities were totally anti-Islamic in nature. Bedouin poetry, in particular, seemed to set him off, whereas, as far as Minah was concerned, poetry was life itself. He used to compose at least five poems every day. His verses were very popular among his friends who kept urging him to take part in the poetry fest. They also kept pressing him to at least participate in the local competitions that took place between the various clans of their own tribe even if he could not go to Okaz. He however did not wish to go against his father's wishes. He would sing his lines to himself when no one else was around. Whenever his mind was troubled, he would venture into the desert alone and, sitting on an *erg* (sand dune), declaim his lines to the desert.

On full moon nights, he would seat himself on sand dunes or hill tops and sing to the moon. Sometimes he would also play the *rubab* (a stringed instrument) secretly. He had his own reasons for keeping his musical forays hidden. Whenever the bedouin tribes held their nightly poetry sessions, he would wrap the end of his *ghutra* (headscarf) around his face to conceal his features and attend the soirees clandestinely. He would often weep bitter tears mourning the fact that he was not allowed to sing on behalf of the al-Zoubi clan. To him, these were not merely poetry competitions but a battle royale among poets. The bedouins believed that these events represented an art form that glorified their culture and showcased their clans' prestige.

Standing in two rows facing one another, the tribesmen would roar in approbation and with raw emotion as poets from the respective sides came forward to recite their *qasidas* (poems). They would encourage each poet from their side with loud shouts of appreciation and support, and spur them on to victory against the opposing team. High on intoxicants, their emotions would also run high and support for the teams would reach such a crescendo that it was not uncommon for trouble to erupt occasionally at such poetry meets.

Rather than stating that they were unaware that the Arab literary world had categorised bedouin poetry as *nabati* (folk writing that does not conform to the classical rules of literary Arabic) and consigned it to the fringes, it would be perhaps be more correct to say that such a classification did not bother them at all. Even though these poems did not conform to the morals and norms specified in their religion, poetry continued to constitute an important part in the bedouin's life.

The poets belonging to both the factions would mentally pay their respects to the *jinns* residing in their souls and pray to them for their blessings to be able to come up with the best poem from inside themselves. They believed that *jinns* belonging to another world enter them and render them capable of composing poems. While some believed that there were *kafir jinns* which came up with secular verses, as opposed to the kind which follow the religious line, bedouin poets saw no differentiation between *jinns*. To them the *jinns* were all unseen, wonderful beings capable of composing great poetry, and the poets were proud that they resided within them. They believed that the spirits had come in search of them and had selected them for the protection of their *kabeela* (tribe). Minah would often weep, ruing the fact that he had been deprived of enjoying this special feeling. Sitting alone on sand dunes, he would lament the fact that he had been unable to bring forth the *jinn* within him and showcase it to the world. He would sit in front of a bonfire and sing a dirge in the sole company of his *jinn*. In the silent expanse of the desert, his lines would float towards the horizon and disperse in the distance.

Some of his friends, who had secretly witnessed these performances, had brought his talent to the notice of the outside world. Impressed with his artistry, the elders of the al-Sodari *faqat (clan)* had requested his father to send him to the poetry competitions. They even went to the extent of asking him to send Minah to the local al-Sodari tribal contests if Ahmed did not wish him to participate in the Okaz festivities. But his father had flatly refused to permit him to take part in any poetry competition at all. He had also made it very clear that he was totally against all such anti-Islamic activities and would never accord his permission for such acts. Despite this pronouncement, Minah continued to occasionally sing to himself. If he felt particularly hurt or depressed, he would hum to himself but, on occasions, his humming would be audible to those around him. That is what happened this time.

As soon as he heard the humming, his elder brother, Saqr picked up a small pebble and threw it at Minah, softly enquiring, "Hey…have you forgotten father is around?" Hamad, the fourth brother, looked at them both and smiled at the exchange.

At seventy, Ahmed ibn Rashid al-Zoubi al-Sodari possessed the acute hearing of an elephant.

"*Meen ya walad?*" (Hey, who's that?) he called out.

No one spoke. He shouted once again, "Who was that?"

The milk spurting from the camels' udders into the vessels provided a unique background score.

A long silence ensued.

Having finished milking his fourth camel, Ahmed ibn Rashid al-Sodari went towards the fifth one.

It was a black camel of the *al mujahim* variety. He was particularly fond of this breed of camels and was still grieving over the loss of the last descendant of the *al mujahim* camel that his grandfather, Saqr ibn Shuja ibn Marri al-Zoubi al-Sodari had brought from Yemen.

Camels were his life and he considered the *jamal* a wondrous gift from God. The only time camels were slaughtered was when guests came visiting. Hospitality to visiting guests was a primary duty of the bedouins. Even if he had only a few scraps to eat himself, visitors must be fed well. For this purpose it didn't matter if he had to sacrifice the camel that he held the dearest. Following this principle, Ahmed ibn Rashid al-Zoubi al-Sodari had on many occasions slaughtered several camels of the *al mujahim* breed that his grandfather had brought over, and served them to his guests.

He shared his grandfather's fondness for the black variety of *al mujahim* camels. His father, Rashid ibn Saqr ibn Shuja al-Sodari however preferred the white breed known as the *al maghatir* camel. Personally he did not care for the white-coloured variety at all. Since his childhood he had been very close to his grandfather…that could very well be the reason for his preference for the *al mujahim* camels.

The black *al mujahim* camel he had affectionately named *Dheeb* had been ailing for over three months. To Ahmed it seemed almost as if his grandfather was himself in agony, and he could not bear the sight of the animal writhing in pain. Despite treatment by several local experts, nothing helped. Finally, his second son had ridden to

RIyadh and brought back an English veterinarian. But his efforts too went in vain. It was no ordinary camel. It could run as fast as a horse and used to vigilantly guard their flock of sheep. One night, when the camel was about three years old, a wolf entered the fold when everyone was fast asleep and attempted to snatch a lamb. It was *Dheeb* who had chased the predator away and thus earned his name: *Dheeb* or 'wolf'. The camel calf that chased a wolf away had been named after the predator itself! Bedouins term a brave person *'dheeb'*, but to Ahmed the camel was more courageous than a wolf and so he personally used to call it '*akhtar min dheeb*' or 'braver than a wolf'.

Dheeb also used to be very fond of Ahmed. It would go out to graze only after it had eaten a few pieces of *khubz* (pita bread) from his hands. It also used to rest its face on Ahmed's shoulder and vocalise, making a characteristic camel sound, as though holding a conversation with him. It seemed to sense and appreciate Ahmed's moods at various points in time and provided him with much solace. Once, when it did not see him for five days at a stretch it simply pined away. One of Ahmed's sons had died in a battle with the Turks. Shattered by the loss, he did not venture out into the desert at all. Following the third day's *hassa* ceremony for the departed soul, and after ensuring that all his relatives and the guests who had come to attend the ceremony had been fed, he took a few pieces of *khubz* and went to Marabidh where the camels were foraging that day. *Dheeb*, which had eaten nothing for four days having not seen Ahmed and was lying supine on the ground, quickly got up when it saw him coming and ran towards him making a soulful, yearning sound typical of camels, called *hanin*. Ahmed stopped in his tracks at the sound. *Dheeb* neared him and wound its long neck around him in an affectionate embrace as though it realised his sorrow, and sought to console him by making another special plaintive call from its throat. *Dheeb*'s mournful *hanin* vocalisation seemed to affect Ahmed more than his son's death and he began weeping bitterly. Perhaps his grief-stricken keening echoed another heart-rending sound made by camels known as *kalooj*, because *Dheeb* which had wrapped its long neck around him also began to shed tears. Given their closeness, he would never have imagined that he would be the one to finally snap the connection between *Dheeb* the *al Mujahim* camel and himself.

He could not bear to see one of the last five *al Mujahim* camels from his grandfather's days suffering in pain due to intestinal ulcers. No treatment seemed to work. When he saw it in agony, he too seemed affected by its pain. He remembered his *sheikh*'s (tribal leader) words that one must kill an animal only if it was absolutely called for, otherwise no animal should be harmed in any manner.

On that day he had picked up his musket and fired a shot at the ailing *Dheeb*. When he saw it fall down on the ground, finally relieved of its pain, Ahmed ibn Rashid al-Zoubi al-Sodari had, for the first time in his adult life, wailed aloud in sorrow.

The painful memory now haunted him. He gathered himself and, having completed his milking, went towards the blanket spread on the ground. As soon as he sat down, his eldest son filled a cup with the camel milk and handed it to him. He drank the milk down, emitted a satisfied burp and said, "*Alhamdulillah!*" He followed it up with four more cups of milk and then asked his sons to drink up as well.

Ahmed ibn Rashid al-Sodari then selected a date from a small bowl, popped it into his mouth and chewed on it appreciatively while looking up at the sky. The rising moon was clearly visible in the rays of the setting sun. Looking at it he began to speak, "When we were young, my elder brother once developed an unbearable itch. My grandfather then gathered some dung from one of the *al Maghatir* camels and applied it on his skin. The itch disappeared within three days…" His sons kept looking at him in anticipation. After a brief silence, he looked at his fourth son Hamad and queried, "It looks like your elder brother has learnt to sing *meshhoob* poetry?" Hamad kept quiet, with his head down, and cast a sidelong glance at Minah. On his part, Minah was trying to breathe quietly. Ahmed looked at him and asked, "When a *al Mujahim* calf went missing and all of you went in different directions to look for it, you were sitting that night on a *thais* (sand dune) and singing….what sort of composition was it? Was it a *meshhoob* or a *majroor*?" This unexpected question threw all his sons into a tizzy.

All of them looked at him in astonishment. Minah softly replied, "It's a new form called the *shella,*" and raised his head to look at his father. Ahmed stared into Minah's eyes and asked, "I'm told you adore the *al Mujahim*?" Minah kept quiet. Ahmed asked again, "The *shella* you hummed today, wasn't it also about the dead *al Mujahim*?" The question seemed to surprise Minah deeply.

K*hozama* flowers seemed to bloom within his heart and he wanted to go up and kiss his father's brow in respect and admiration. He merely looked at him and nodded quietly in assent.

Nodding his head in return, Ahmed ibn Rashid al-Sodari, ate a few more dates and continued, "My mother was a very good *meshhoob* singer herself. She had a favourite lamb. When it had to be slaughtered to feed some guests, she composed a *meshhoob* in its memory the next day. It made me and my sister cry when we heard it…." Saying this he looked smilingly at Minah whose eyes teared up.

"When is the next camel race at Mizaein?" he dropped another bombshell at his stunned sons as he removed a date seed from his mouth.

His eldest son said in a faint voice, "It's tomorrow…."

Ahmed asked, "Will the al-Sodari *kazzama* camel win again this time also?" and eagerly awaited the reply.

A moment's deep silence.

"Well? I'm waiting for a reply…." he asked irritatedly.

Hamid ventured softly, "*Labbe....*"

"I asked if we'll win again this time around also...." his anger bubbled to the surface.

Softly Hamid answered, "The *kazzama* camel died a few months ago...." and attempted to avoid his father's glare.

Ahmed's eyes widened with surprise. "*Inna Lillahi wa inna ilayhi raji'un* (Indeed we belong to Allah, and indeed to Him we shall return)....Why wasn't I told earlier?" He had found a new grouse to rail against. No one spoke a word.

But Minah responded softly, "The whole town was grief-stricken. Hundreds of *mankoos* (folk) songs echoed all around. Many people mourned and even fasted for days on end. You were then in holy Makkah for the *hajj*. No one had the courage to break the news to you when you returned....." Having had his quick say, he looked at Ahmed apprehensively.

Ahmed stared at the ground for a while and then asked, "If so, which camel is going to represent our *kabeela* at the races?" Minah thought he discerned the sharpness of a *jambiya* (dagger) in that question.

The eldest son responded, "The *maghatir* camel of the al-Mulaqims...."

The desert wind suddenly seemed to pick up. Ahmed exhaled noisily and addressed his sons, "Mmmm....I want all of you to attend the race this time. And Minah, I want you to sing a beautiful poem in praise of our Sodari camel and impress everyone....." At this, Minah, visibly overcome, placed his forefinger on the tip of his nose and acknowledged the instruction humbly saying, "*Alakasham*," to which Ahmed responded by saying, "*Alashsheham*."

Whether it was camel racing or poetry competition, this was the first time Ahmed had permitted his sons to attend any of these events. It was his belief that bedouins acted in a maniacal fashion at such events and he did not want his sons to indulge in such activities.

His stand was that these events, which only helped provoke internecine strife among the bedouins, were anti-Islamic and should therefore be completely avoided. It was Islam which had spread peace among us. The religion had been born solely to eradicate the wars, bloodshed, hatred and feelings of vengeance that had existed among the bedouins for centuries….instead of promoting the tenets of peace, harmony and brotherhood that the religion was trying to teach us, should we continue to squabble amongst ourselves like our forefathers before us? That was an uncivilised way of life…..And the poetry….what did it really amount to? Singing the praises of one's own *kabeela* or *faqat*…. songs that were self-aggrandising and glorified bloodthirsty events, bragging that we fought such and such a battle, we won that war and defeated our enemies badly, we slaughtered our opponents…."won't such poems only end up fostering more hatred, anger and infighting among the *kabeelas*?" he would fume. His constant complaint was that poetry also fostered improper thoughts such as love and corporeal fulfilment and these topics needed to be weeded out totally. But today, either setting aside all such prejudices or giving them up altogether, he was urging his sons to participate in the camel race. He had a grand plan in mind.

His long-standing ambition was to put an end to the centuries-long enmity between the al-Zoubi and the al-Mulaqim clans of the al-Sodari tribe. That was the reason why he had urged his son to sing a paean in praise of the al-Mulaqim camel. Plus he had another design at the back of his mind. He often felt that such gestures were unavoidable if the Ottoman army was to be prevented from intruding into Arabia's Najd area and the unity of the bedouins of Najd was to be preserved. This coming together would also help the spread of the true teachings of Islam by fostering unity among the *bedus*. Since the bedouins of west Arabia had allied themselves with the

Ottomans, there was every possibility that the Turks would attack Najd for the third time any day now. If all the clans were to unite under the leadership of Diriyah's Emir to resist the Turks' offensive such gatherings of *bedus* were indispensable. The Emir of Diriyah's hands need to be strengthened if we are to drive the Turks back. The path shown to us by Al Bavah (a religious reformer) was the true Islamic path and we should strive to implement it throughout the land. The *bedus* who were reverting to the pre-Islamic *jahiliyyah* period (a time of ignorance or barbarism in Islamic history) needed to be curbed and brought back to the true Islamic path once again. The feelings of enmity and violence among the *bedus* and all the attendant vices needed to be eradicated and the true teachings of Islam such as peace, brotherhood and universal love should once again be re-established in this land. Some *bedus* still continued to worship stones and trees despite being persuaded to the contrary. A few still persist in illicit sexual relationships ....not just with the opposite sex....my God, it's unspeakable to just think about these things....Al Bavah's teachings about the correct Islamic path are the only means to set them straight.

The Emir and Al Bavah had previously come together to bring back the proper Islamic lifestyle to Arabia. In Baghdad there are people who worship at the mausoleums of Imams. They also burst into song and inflict pain upon themselves. This seems to be their version of religion! As though that were not enough, there are some here who swear by *jinns*. Al Bavah and the Emir managed to bring all these people to the right path, but the Turks came here bringing with them their own version of Islam. If things were to be set straight, the Turks need to be chased out of our land. To achieve this, the *bedus* need to be united. In order to thwart the Turks' ambition of annexing the whole of Arabia if the *bedus* can all come together in the name of Islam, that would also pave the way for everyone to follow the true religious path. This would also give rise to a new country where strict laws prescribing harsh punishments can be formulated to bring the unruly *bedu* to heel. All the false gods of the *jahiliyya* period would then be automatically eradicated. I hear Queen Victoria of England has turned her subjects into a moral and disciplined lot. We need to do the same. We need to enforce draconian laws in order to transform these immoral persons into righteous Muslims. Like Queen Victoria enforces her religion in her country, let us implement the correct form of Islam here. Let us learn from her how she reformed her religion and enforce our methods here. But first, the Turks need to be ejected from our territory.

We may have suffered two defeats at their hands. We should not fail a third time. The Emir of Diriyah would certainly ensure this. A few of our clansmen refuse to accept the leadership of the Diriyah *bedus* and strengthen the Emir's hands. I fear that if we continue this game of one-upmanship, it would only benefit the enemy ultimately.

Some members of our clan do not like our alliance with the British against the Turks. Perhaps they are against their modern weaponry - the guns and the cannons - that are being employed in the battles? Are they worried that these weapons could be used by some *bedus* to subjugate other bedouins, giving their community's traditions the go-by, and that is why they are refusing to fight against the Turks? Or, are they of the view, that with the never-ending squabbles among the *bedus* themselves, the Turkish incursions are of little consequence? In their eyes is the internal enemy worse than the external one? Or, are they apprehensive that some bedouin clans could grow stronger due to their alliance with the British and end up lording it over the others? Are they worried that the British are stuffing the bedouins' brains with religious frenzy? Is that why they refuse to heed the call for coming together to assist in the war against the common enemy? No….we do need to come together and unite as one. This camel race is the ideal opportunity. I'll send my sons to attend it….my second son, Saeed will also accompany them. They will mind him and moderate their behaviour. Yes, he definitely needs to go with them….

As these thoughts ran through Ahmed ibn Rashid ibn Saqr al-Zoubi al-Sodari's mind, the time for the *maghrib* prayers was nearing.

While the third war with the Turks was occupying his mind, he had absolutely no inkling of the impending First World War that was looming on the horizon.

That night Minah was preparing to attend the camel race at Mizaein along with his brothers. He was feeling elated at having been given the opportunity to unleash upon the world the *jinn* that resided within him all these years.

4

Rajendran clutched at Palani's feet and pleaded piteously.

"On my mother's head I promise I didn't steal that bag *anna*.... I know nothing about that Arab's bag....please believe me Palani *anna* ...."

Palani raised Rajendran up and sat him down.

"Don't believe him *anna*....he's faking it...."

Without responding to Sundar's words, Palani kept gazing at Rajendran.

No one said a word. Rajendran shook his head slightly and let out a small belch. That sound seemed to offend Sundar's ears.

He aimed a kick at Rajendran.

"Sit down Sundar....you know he has this habit of burping constantly...." Palani shouted angrily.

Palani was easily the eldest among those present. He came from a village near Madurai in South India and had spent some twenty-five years of his life at the town of Al Sulayyil in the Najd region of Saudi Arabia. He had been invited to preside over the inquiry regarding the theft case as he was well aware of Saudi Arabia's earlier and current laws and regulations, and had also carried out extensive research into the minutiae of Bedouin life and customs. He knew how to comport himself among the three different categories of Arabs and was considered by many Tamils as perhaps the very first Tamilian to arrive at the Najd region. He was well-known to Tamilians in all the surrounding towns and was the first man they would approach if a countryman was in any trouble. He was reputed to have inside influence ranging from the *jawazat* (Immigration Department) to the *shurta* (police), and it was a matter of pride for Sundar and Rajendran that a man with such a *wasta* (clout) resided on the same street as them.

"Palani *anna*....don't be fooled by him....just scroll through his mobile and you'll realise what sort of a person he really is....do you know he has pornographic videos on it despite my warning him several times that he could be arrested for them? Forget that, do you know what he did just last month? When you were away on vacation, he met up with Sivakumar - you know, that fellow who lives near the camel *souk* - and both got drunk on illicit arrack ...."

"Don't you know the police arrested all those involved in illicit hooch distilling last month itself?" Palani tried to assert his superior authority and influence.

"Forget that....ask him yourself....if he had been nabbed by the police who is supposed to answer his parents? As it is, his family and mine don't get along very well back home. If something untoward happens to him, who would be held responsible for it?" Sundar's tone became defensive. To counter it, Rajendran immediately turned to Palani and responded bravely, "Nothing like that is likely to happen.... even if it does, wouldn't Palani *annan* take care of matters?" When he heard these words, Palani got flustered and, with a view to hiding his apprehension, burst out angrily, "Forget it, you son of a bitch....if you drag my name into any of your shenanigans, I'll personally pull your tongue out." Taking advantage of this opportunity, an emboldened Sundar got a burst of fresh energy and again appealed to Palani, "See Palani *anna*? Look how callous this fellow is? And you said he was just a kid and couldn't have stolen the bag…."

Scared that he might get into trouble himself if he allowed matters to drag on, Palani turned to Rajendran and said decisively, "Look, I give you two days' time….if you come up with the truth by the evening of the day after tomorrow, I'll deal with you leniently….otherwise, your cousin says he wants to go to the police….you know the law of this land, don't you? It's not like our country….you'll be beaten to a pulp…..it's not a simple matter. You've stolen the property of an Arab….it's now up to you…." Having delivered the ultimatum, he rose from his seat and began to walk away.

Sundar followed him.

Rajendran kept looking at them.

While he was gazing after Sundar with some surprise at not having been locked up inside his room, Sundar turned and yelled out to him, "Hey! Go and open the garage for business….I've to attend to a vehicle in the *sahraa* (desert) and will be back only in the afternoon or latest by the *maghrib salah* (the fourth prayer of the day)....the two Hindi-speaking guys will get here only at 10 o' clock….got it?"

Something in Sundar's tone of voice - was it affection or fraternal love? - seemed to affect the grunt that emanated from Rajendran's throat in response to these instructions.

As Sundar went on his way, Rajendran momentarily stood there feeling that his gait was a sad one, and wondered sadly whether he was unnecessarily tormenting his cousin.

As soon as he disappeared, he took a shower, dabbed on some anti-perspirant and started out.

The garage on the next street awaited his arrival.

At the entrance to the garage stood the jeep belonging to that Arab, Shuja ibn Saqr al-Zoubi al-Sodari. It was his bag that Rajendran was alleged to have stolen.

Rajendran's stomach roiled at the sight of the Arab's vehicle.

Two North Indians, his workmates, were awaiting his arrival.

As he pushed up the shutters to the garage, his hands trembled.

"Ya Rashendra....*ta'al hina* (come here)," Shuja called out from inside the jeep.

Rajendran approached him with dragging feet. After staring at him unblinkingly for a short while, Shuja ordered, ""*Erkab ya Rajjal* (get in, young man)."

Rajendran felt his innards quaking.

"Get in the car," commanded the bedouin Arab Shuja in a loud tone again. Rajendran climbed into the Land Cruiser and sat down.

5

Every line spouted by Minah was being received with loud shouts of acclaim by the huge, adoring crowd which then echoed them back resoundingly. All the various clans belonging to the al-Sodari tribe were escorting their fancied camel amidst much fanfare. Many of them also followed the entourage on their horses and camels. It was the camel beauty pageant. Bedouins from all over Arabia attend this annual competition which showcases their prettiest camels. Apart from races, the annual event also included a beauty competition in which the most beautiful camels participated. It was this beauty pageant that was the highlight of the proceedings and attracted more attention than the camel races themselves.

Four elders were entrusted with the responsibility of judging the camels' looks. They would select the most beautiful camel based on criteria such as the length of its neck, drooping lips, the height and shape of the hump, a long nose and ears that stood back. Camel aesthetics are evaluated according to precise categories determined generations ago.

For the past ten years it has been the *kazzama* camel belonging to the al-Sodaris that has been consistently winning these beauty competitions.

It was an extraordinary animal, a true ship of the desert brought straight down from the heavens. No other camel in Arabia had been able to get the better of it for the last ten years. Just to watch it sashay up to the winners' circle year after year was enough to send the al-Sodaris into a frenzy of delight.

The term *kazzama* itself literally meant "in-your-face" and, for the past ten years, it lived up to its name by shredding the reputation of all the other tribes to pieces. When the *kazzama* swayed on its way among the adoring crowds, the young men belonging to the al-Sodari tribe used to accompany it to much cheering, shouting and singing poems composed in its and their tribe's praise. Such was the crowd and its adulation that it would take a minimum of three hours for the animal to make its way to the judges' circle. The men would yell slurs calculated to make the opposing tribesmen bristle, and declaim poetry, made up on the spur of the moment, loudly enough to rent the skies. Some would be so transported with joy that they would be jumping up and down maniacally, kissing the champion camel making strange, incoherent sounds all the while. Their yells would reach the stars, "No one can beat us this year either….it is *kazzama* all the way once again…."

But this battle cry was missing this year. Even though the *kazzama* camel's death had handed them a setback, they had come this year with a new camel and the same old fervour. The same rallying cries, the same spirit, the same prancing…..but the earlier intensity seemed to be missing.

As the al-Mulaqim clan's camel was being held up to be the entire al-Sodari tribe's pride, the tribesmen echoed Minah's lines so it resounded in every direction. And as he kept composing newer and better lines spontaneously, Minah became certain of one thing: he concluded that, as was generally believed, a *jinn* inside of him was the cause of the wonder, that was poetry, to spring forth from within him.

He kept on producing and singing his lines thinking all the while, 'I'm sure that a *jinn* inside of me is spouting poetry from within me, and I should somehow discover it'.

Some bedouin poets believe in this idea. They take pride in the belief that a *jinn* within their bodies produces the poetry that comes out of their mouths, and desperately wish to connect with that illusory spirit. They would swear by the legend that these poetry-inspiring *jinns* inhabit an unseen, imaginary land called *Abqer Wadi*. According to them, these *jinns* would occasionally leave *Abqer Wadi* and enter into human bodies in order to reveal the world of poetry to us. Several men had gone in search of the mythical city of *Abqer Wadi,* whose very air was filled with poetry. Many bedouin poets have searched for that land of poetry from Arabia to Iraq and from Yemen to Morocco, all across deserts, dense forests, rivers and hills, but the city has continued to remain elusive.

The mystical *Abqer Wadi* expanded and took shape within Minah's heart. Simultaneously the desert began infiltrating into his soul. A wondrous feeling overcame his body. The desert was the ideal location for a poet like him....there was nothing to hinder his imagination from running wild in all that wide open space. It was a free and unhindered place, an independent world of its own....it was not constrained by any human limitations or by false notions of morality and ethics. It reflected extraordinary images rarely seen in human life. You can actually hear a flower bloom here. It is an endless space containing illusory mirages. It is totally different from the world as we know it. That is where you will discover a different world inhabited by *jinns*. The occupants of that world may even now be alongside us at this very instant. Just as the *jinn* inside of me is spouting poetry and creating a flood of magical words, there may be other spirits inside other men creating similar magic as well.....as this thought struck him, his eyes scanned the crowds.

The entire crowd was moving with the camel and keeping pace with its progress. Minah kept on singing his lines and walking with the crowd. It was then that he noticed that a man on a horse, his face covered by his *ghutrah*, was watching him keenly. Minah saw that the person, riding a fine Arabian horse, was intermittently glancing at his legs. However hard he looked, he could not make out the man's face or any other identifying feature for, apart from covering his face, the man had also wrapped a dark blanket around himself in order to appear indistinguishable. Even though he dismissed him initially as another al-Sodari *bedu*, his suspicions began to soar. To provoke the man further, he racked his brains and came up with lines that no one had thought of before about the glory of the al-Sodari tribe and their attachment to camels that plunged everyone around him into absolute ecstasy. His ringing voice drew everyone's attention to him.

After every two lines Minah would direct his attention towards the mysterious horseman as he kept pace with the rest of the crowd. He was also watching out for weapons the man might be carrying either in his waist or on his back. He kept singing his inspired lines even as he was mentally calculating which of his own swords he should deploy in case the man launched a sudden attack on him. His head reeled as these developments gave him a sudden rush.

When at last the camel reached the circle in front of the judges, the Sodari youth in the crowd let out loud shouts and jumped about in exultation.

The *al Maghatir* camel, relishing the crowd's approbation, paced the circle slowly, bobbing its long neck gracefully, and walked around delicately with mincing steps as though performing a minuet. As it moved its mouth its lips seemed to flutter in the wind and this sight sent the al-Sodaris into transports of delight once again. As it entered the judging circle, it seemed to the onlookers as though the animal's nose had grown longer and it caused them to yell delightedly, "*Kasham*....

ya rajhil....kasham." *Kasham* in Arabic refers to the nose. Among the bedouins the nose occupies a very important place. Equating human life with the nose, they would enquire about each other's well-being while touching their noses. Also if someone they respected asked a favour of them, they would demonstrate that they considered such a task more valued than their life itself by placing their index finger on their nose and saying, "*Alakasham.*" Similarly, they look at a camel's nose to determine its beauty. The nose should be proportionate to the size of its head and should droop down.

The white camel stood still in the centre of the circle. The shouts and slogans slowly died down and a silence descended upon the crowd. While some looked at the judges' eyes, others gazed apprehensively at the camel's legs. The al-Sodaris were suddenly gripped with fear. If the camel decided to squat or lie down on the ground, the game was over - they would lose the contest. One al-Sodari tribesman thumped his thighs in challenge and let out a cry, "It's a pure-bred, genuine camel....it doesn't know the meaning of fear just like us.... *Akhu Noora* (a challenge).....we'll win this time around also...."

Many in the crowd feared that the camel, tired out after a three to four hour walk, might slump down in exhaustion.

Everyone's eyes were now focussed on the yet-to-be-named camel's legs. Its name would depend upon how well it performed at today's event.

Still upright, the *al Maghatir* camel belonging to the *al-Mulaqims* swayed its neck sinuously, slowly put its front right leg forward, moved to the left corner of the circle, stopped and glanced at its owner making a slight sound in its throat. The owner, in a calming gesture, made pacifying noises such as "ooov.....whoov....irrraa....irraa.... drrrrrru......whoov.....drrrrrru....whoov... in soothing camel-speak to the animal.

Immediately Minah recited a few lines that touched the listeners' hearts and filled the Sodaris' throats. As though drawn by the words, the camel slowly stepped out of the circle's boundary. The Sodaris welcomed the move with a loud yell. Tears filled everyone's eyes. Its owner rained kisses on its face and hugged its legs exultantly. Minah then recited some extraordinary verses that stunned all the listeners. The camel's owner, and a sworn enemy of the al-Zoubi clan, Mathar ibn Ibrahim, who was astounded at Minah's facility at versification, as though anticipating every move of his camel, spontaneously gave Minah a tight hug and planted an appreciative kiss on his forehead. At this rare sight of two unlikely poles uniting, all the al-Sodaris shouted in approbation welcoming the gesture.

At that moment, a *bedu* belonging to the al-Mulaqims let out a mocking laugh and loudly exclaimed, "Their great-grandfather was a low life scum married to a harlot…..all this drama of reciting poetry is nothing but a charade." As soon as they heard these words, men belonging to both the al-Zoubi and the al-Mulaqim clans were incensed and rushed forward to grab hold of him.

Before any of them could reach him, a dagger thrown by someone in the crowd pierced his throat. A scuffle broke out even before the culprit could be identified. The area resembled a battleground between the al-Zoubis and the al-Mulaqims who had been united all this while.

"We ourselves would have chastised him….how could you kill one of ours?"

"This was a pre-planned incident meant to insult us in front of all the *bedus* in Arabia….."

As words that flew thick and fast in the dust and sand quickly morphed into swords, daggers, spears and muskets, Minah stood there stunned in the crowd.

Minah had noticed where the dagger that flew in the air and silenced the man had come from. It was the mystery man on the horseback, whom he had suspected of stalking him, who had thrown the knife. It was the same man who had his face covered in the *luthma* using his headscarf who had hurled the knife and killed the man from the opposing clan who had insulted their *faqat*. He had erroneously assumed that the man was after him. He too must be an al-Zoubi. As Minah was caught up in all these conflicting thoughts, someone swiftly pulled him up onto a horse and started galloping away. Minah had been gathered up in one swoop and, seating him behind him, the person had begun riding away hard. He looked back but could see no one. The horse was negotiating the desert smoothly and effortlessly. Minah extended his neck forward and peered to see who had saved him from the melee ....Oh!

It was that man....the same man he had his suspicions about....he was the person who had killed their clan's detractor in one swoop....

"Stop....stop...who're you? Where are you taking me? *Thaqfa.... thaqfa....*" Minah shouted out. *Thaqfa* was a word used by a bedouin in times of mortal danger and, when uttered, the other bedouins would rush immediately to the assistance of the person invoking that word. That was the word Minah was uttering now. Only this time there was no one around to answer his desperate call. Gathering his wits, Minah tried to pull at the *luthma* around his abductor's face to catch a glimpse of his face. The man evaded Minah's attempts to remove his face covering. Minah persisted in his efforts and, as both squirmed and bucked, the horse stumbled and both men fell to the ground. The horse too fell but recovered and stood up with shaking legs. Minah fumbled for the sword at his waist. It had fallen down somewhere in the scuffle. He pulled out his dagger and thrust it towards the man's eyes.

The man removed the *luthma* around his face and displayed his face.

Minah stood absolutely stunned.

It was his father, Ahmed ibn Rashid al-Zoubi al-Sodari!

Was this the same man who railed strongly against the violence prevalent in a bedouin's life? Hadn't he sent us to the camel races so that we could get along peaceably with the al-Mulaqim clan? Was it this same man? Was this the man who kept preaching to us to give up violence and follow the peaceful path of our religion? Was it impossible to ever get rid of the bloodthirst inherent in a *bedu*'s heart?

As Minah stared at him in stunned silence, Ahmed ibn Rashid al-Zoubi al-Sodari pronounced:

"If your enemy is as brave and capable as you, you should honour him. If he insults you in his cowardice, you should immediately lop his head off."

6

"Which part of India are you from - Kerala, U.P. or Madras?" Shuja ibn Saqr al-Zoubi al-Sodari asked Rajendran. That was the conversation starter. For his part, Rajendran was feeling pretty chuffed about travelling with an Arab in his Land Cruiser MUV for the very first time.

"Madras."

"How long have you been here?"

'Two and a half...."

As he responded automatically, Rajendran was suddenly reminded of the dream. What a coincidence! I'm actually travelling in a car with a *bedu* exactly like in my dream! It seems grandmother was right after all - dreams that occur during the early morning hours apparently do come true!

The Arab was asking something he couldn't follow.

Shuja repeated his question again more clearly:

"Didn't you go to school in India? Is your family very poor? I'm told schooling is very expensive in India. Is that true?"

"No, boss....government schools there are not all that expensive...."

"Then why didn't you continue your studies?"

"I wasn't very good at studies...."

"You're lying, right? Your parents pulled you out of school and sent you here so you can earn some money. Am I correct? I hear there are a lot of poor people in India...."

"It was not that, boss. I was truly bad at studies. And we can't be classified as poor either. We own three acres of land. Earlier we used to own a lot more, but lost most of it. Among all our relatives, our family owned the most land. Unable to stomach that, someone in our own family cheated us of most of it....my great-grandfather was murdered by somebody....we still haven't figured out who....I believe he used to pick fights in the name of our caste at the slightest provocation...."

What's 'caste'?"

"It's like you have bedouins, *hadaris* and *asmar* (Black Arabs) here.... can I say something, boss?"

"*Faddal....*"

"I swear I didn't steal your bag...."

"What bag?"

"The one you were angrily questioning my cousin about at the garage yesterday...."

"Oh, that! Hahaha...I did that only to scare him....your cousin is a thieving dog....that's why....*kalli valli* (forget it)....but what's *your* beef with him? I've seen the two of you arguing and, even though I don't understand your language, I get the impression that you two do not get along at all...."

"He's *majnun* (crazy), boss....I don't like working with him, but what can I do? It's my fate...."

"Mmmm.....do one thing....I'm planning to open a *jawaal* (cell phone) shop, *Insha'allah*....come and work for me there...."

"Oh, thank you boss. Please let me have your mobile number."

"I'll personally come and take you there....work there for some time."

"Thank you, boss....can I say one more thing? You appeared in my dream last night...."

"*Wallahi*?"

"Yes, boss....honestly you did...."

At that, Shuja stopped the vehicle and smilingly got off without mentioning that Rajendran had in turn appeared in *his* dream. He took his leave after asking Rajendran to keep the MUV safely at the garage until his return.

Rajendran was absolutely on cloud nine. This was the first time he was driving an Arab's Land Cruiser. His heart thundered with elation.

Hey Sundar...It's a pity you aren't here to see this....wait and watch, I'll teach you a lesson you won't forget in a hurry....I am now friends with an Arab.....and he's no ordinary Arab, he's a *bedu*....who's not scared of anything....who is a straight-shooter with honest folk and a terror to crooks....he knows fully well you are an utter fraud...."

Onlookers would assume that an Arab was behind the wheels of the four-wheel-drive....

Rajendran drove the vehicle with panache.

The vehicle stopped at a signal. He spotted a few policemen conducting traffic checks. A feeling of dread spread through his body. Keeping his phone on the dashboard, he quickly executed a right turn.

As he drove through the side roads of Sulayyil, something nudged his foot. He picked it up. It was a plastic package whose contents were not visible. He put it in his shirt pocket. Could it be 'that'?

Some persons dealt with 'that' illegally in this country. They must be real foolhardy to try something like that....if they were caught, they could be awarded the death penalty and beheaded in public. And in spite of this, they still distribute 'that'. Nah! I don't think it's 'that'.

Still, let me hang on to it...what if it *was* 'that'? I'll show it to Sivakumar *annan.* He'll surely know about it...he's the expert on hooch, marijuana and 'that'....

Oh, yes! Now I remember....I was told that guy, Mehboob Khan from Bihar committed suicide after downing a large dose of 'that'....Poor fellow! Apparently he had family problems back home....his mother and wife were constantly squabbling....and his wife finally ran off with another man....unable to bear the humiliation he had committed suicide. It was reported that he also had financial problems.... he was apparently struggling to repay the million rupee loan he had taken to construct his house.... As though that wasn't enough, his wife is said to have taken with her whatever little jewellery was left in the house when she ran off....But don't they say that suicide is a grave sin in Islam....and no true Muslim would consider such an act? If so, why did Mehboob Khan take this extreme step? Perhaps the rule does not apply to Indian Muslims....?

Poor Mehboob Khan....his entire life was filled with tragedy....he had come to Saudi Arabia just one year after his marriage, thinking he was to be employed here as a driver....but he had been hoodwinked by the employment agent in Mumbai. He had actually come to this country on a gardener's visa and, within two days of his arrival, his *kafeel* (sponsor) had sent him into the desert to herd camels in the company of an Ethiopian.

Faced initially with a lot of difficulties in settling down, Mehboob Khan slowly began assimilating the different weather patterns of the desert. The Arab sponsor who would drop in at their place of work once a week would bring them bread, water and snacks. As days went by, Mehboob found it increasingly difficult to cope with the desert's heat, dust, cold and silence. He planned to somehow escape from the place. Initially he had second thoughts about this plan upon hearing the horror stories related by the Ethiopian. Memories of his wife's magnetic body kept tormenting him until one night he finally decided to make his way out of the hell-hole wishing to at least hear her voice one more time. He had absolutely no idea which direction to head to reach the nearest city in the vast expanse of the desert. The Ethiopian had also warned him, "The desert is a dangerous place. You cannot run or hide anywhere. Unless you are endowed with God's blessings, you cannot survive even two nights in it on your own....by the second day itself your body will have dissolved into the sand. Thirsting for water, your body will begin to ooze blood..... the wandering desert *jinns* will be waiting to take possession of your body....no, my Indian friend, don't even think of leaving.... You'll die a horrible death...."

Wherever he looked there were only sand dunes....forget humans, not even a stray camel was in sight. The supply of water and snacks he had packed for the trip was exhausted. Three nights had passed since his escape. He thought back about the Ethiopian's words and felt like weeping. The man had been right in his assessment, but, even if Mehboob wanted to return, how was he now supposed to find his way back? He remembered the Ethiopian saying that the desert kept shifting its shape and its landscape changed from day to day. Yes indeed! What he had said was the literal truth....surviving in the desert was an arduous process....it not only required a strong body but also a resolute mind. When he wondered how the bedouins managed to survive in this harsh environment, his head reeled and he had fallen into a faint. His keenness to somehow get back home and give his wife a thrashing to set her right fell by the wayside just like his unclaimed body that lay in the middle of the desert.

When he opened his eyes someone was standing in front of him. Startled, he rose, rubbed his eyes and looked again. The man introduced himself as a Pakistani driver of a water tanker, and gave him a ride up to the main road. He advised Mehboob to hitchhike from that spot to the nearest town, and left after thrusting a hundred riyal note on him.

This is how Mehboob Khan had reached Al Sullayil, the town where Rajendran was employed, and started his second innings there. He had secured a job in a local *mazra* (farm) and slept peacefully for the first time since his arrival in Saudi Arabia. Rajendran had met Mehboob when he had gone to the *mazra* once on a work-related visit and had got to hear his story.

After a few months, just as Mehboob was preparing to go back to India for a holiday, that devastating news reached him. The report that his wife had run off with another man threw him totally off balance, led him to ramble aimlessly in the desert and ultimately jump into an abandoned borewell hole and end his life.

As he recalled this story of Mehboob Khan from Bihar, a nameless fear enveloped Rajendran. Mehboob's handsome face appeared before his mind's eye and gave him the jitters. He recalled the moment when Mehboob had likened him to Salman Khan, a Bollywood matinee idol, and how thrilled he had felt at the comparison. The fright he felt focussed his attention back to the package in his pocket.

What if it contained drugs and he was caught by the police with it in his possession….!?

He quickly tossed the packet out of the window.

Immediately he felt a pang of regret for having thrown it away. It couldn't have been drugs, could it?….It was not all that easy to obtain drugs in this country.....they have to be smuggled in clandestinely from abroad....apparently some Afghanis, Indians, Pakistanis and Bangladeshis sneak them in.....they must be truly desperate to do so despite knowing that the punishment for drug smuggling was death by beheading.....

He now felt like laughing when he recalled his saying once to Sivakumar *annan* only half-seriously, "*Anna*, why don't we also get into the drug trade?" Even though it was said partly in jest, wasn't it true that I had once entertained that thought?

Just thinking on those lines was wrong....a fatal mistake....if caught, the police would behead the offender in public.

Only a few years ago four men belonging to Bangladesh had had their heads cut off. This incident took place before I arrived here. It was said that all the four had been engaged in the drug trade.

I wonder what the punishment would be for those two Malayalees and the Tamilian recently caught distilling illicit liquor? Would they also be beheaded?

I shouldn't have gone there with Sivakumar *annan*.

A formless fear enveloped Rajendran once again. His vision seemed to blur. He brought the vehicle to a halt. His heart began to beat fast. Despite the heat outside, a sort of change was visible. The garage was quite close by. He switched off the ignition, lowered the window and peered outside.

Dark clouds were beginning to gather.

Two Pakistanis were passing by and one was remarking to the other in Urdu, "Normally the rains only come after winter.....this year, however, they seem to be setting in earlier...." These words entered Rajendran's ears and frightened him for some reason. His heart began to beat rapidly.

There were signs that an *obaar* (sand storm) was brewing and coming in from the desert towards the town. Rajendran started the Land Cruiser and engaged the gears.

As he changed into second gear, he observed the approaching sandstorm and drove faster.

As the MUV stopped in front of the garage, the *obaar* struck.

The fear inside him now reminded him of the dream he had last night.

Didn't Raghu *mama* also appear in it along with that bedouin? He had said something then….what was it? Did he call me a criminal *maplai*?

Had Sundar called home and slandered me?

All my relatives would be taunting *amma*….they would ask her sarcastically, "You were boasting about your son going abroad and earning good money….is this how he makes his living?" and laugh mockingly. "He was a wastrel while he was here, and now he's a thief over there……" they would goad her.

Appa would be humiliated….he'd shed tears and wail, "My only son has turned out to be a thief….."

Sundar, if you have filled their ears with slander about me, rest assured I'll not spare you….if need be, I'll not even hesitate to kill you…..

7

Ahmed ibn Rashid al-Zoubi al-Sodari's grandfather, Saqr ibn Shuja ibn Marri ibn Saqr ibn Bandar ibn Shuja ibn Marri al-Zoubi al-Sodari, was returning home after planting palm saplings in his grove. The land at the foothills of Jebel Tuwaiq had come down to him over generations. It was a portion of land belonging to the al-Zoubi clan of the al-Sodari tribe that had originally fallen to the lot of his great-great-great-grandfather. His great-great-great-grandfather had also been named Saqr. It was common practice among bedouins to name their sons after their grandfathers and great-grandfathers. And it was also usual to append to it the names of their father, grandfather, great-grandfather, great-great-grandfather, his father and so on for up to sixteen generations. It was during their sixth generation that the al-Sodaris had converted to Islam. The previous generations used to worship Jebel Tuwaiq, the mountain that stood like a sentinel to their grove, as their god. But not any longer. After they turned to Islam, they had given up their pagan rituals and adopted the Islamic true path prescribed by the Almighty. Many bedouins had also given up their nomadic habits, settled down at fixed abodes and became agriculturists, dividing up the land among themselves. It was claimed that their hostilities and blood lust had diminished after the advent of Islam.

But Saqr ibn Shuja ibn Marri al-Zoubi al-Sodari had also heard it said that, despite turning to Islam over a thousand years ago, the *bedus* had not entirely given up all their previous habits. Two hundred years before the bedouins of Diriyah routed the Turkish army and established a new kingdom called Saudi Arabia, the protagonist of this Chapter, Saqr ibn Shuja ibn Marri ibn Saqr ibn Bandar ibn Shuja ibn Marri al-Zoubi al-Sodari was riding home on his horse mulling over plans for the banquet he was hosting the next day and the manner in which his guests needed to be received. A *sheikh* of the al-Zoubi clan of the Sodari tribe, he was a true believer.

Some twenty years back, he had reacted furiously when some of the tribesmen of their clan had deviated from the true path of Islam and regressed to the tribal practices belonging to the age of the *jahiliyyah*. In consultation with some of the *faqats* in his *kabeela*, he was striving to bring them back to the fold of Islam once again.

Many years back a religious battle had erupted at Diriyah in the Najd province of Arabia. Saqr had been a very young man when the Emir of Diriyah declared holy war against the *bedus* who had renounced Islam and reverted to the age of the *jahiliyyah,* ending up worshipping their false gods. He had then lent his wholehearted support to the *jihad* upon learning that the Emir had waged the spiritual struggle with the active support of a true Islamic religious reformer. Later, when the Emir of Diriyah launched an all-out war to oust the Ottomans who had occupied Arabia, specially the holy cities of Mecca and Medina, he had not only sent warriors from his tribe to strengthen the Emir's hands but had also participated in the battles himself. He had striven hard to lay siege to the Ottoman-occupied province of Hejaz, drive the invaders out of the holy cities and annex the territories back into Arabia. But, five years ago, when Turkish forces had once again invaded and captured Arabia, he had lost the will to fight. He had however deputed his sons to fight in the resultant war. When two of them were captured by the Turks and taken to Istanbul as prisoners of war, all he could feel was impotent sorrow and intense anger. He could do nothing to avenge the act. Even though two of his sons had been killed by the Turks, he felt a sense of pride in their sacrifice. He would relate stories to his grandchildren about his valiant sons who had laid down their lives for the sake of their religion, and take great pride in their achievement. It was his practice to send all the children of the household to *mullahs* (religious teachers) in order that they may grow up following the true Islamic path by learning all the rules laid down in their religion. Simultaneously, he had reacted with fury to some clans of the al-Sodari tribe worshipping trees and certain heathen gods known as *Al Uzza* that existed during the times of the *jahiliyyah,* and had personally gone into the desert and chopped down the offending trees. He fumed that instead of adhering to the morality, ethics and rules of good behaviour prescribed in Islam, his people were indulging in intoxicants, worshipping inanimate objects, such as trees and mountains and following a dissolute lifestyle. He kept insisting that the way of Islam was the ideal one for all humankind and that they should renounce the immoral ways of the *jahiliyyah* once and for all and return to Islam's fold. It was as an extension to this campaign that he was hosting the banquet at his home the next day.

He was on his way home after overseeing the planting of new date palm saplings in his grove and after instructing the black slaves there, who had been in his family for generations, to water them carefully.

Even while he was blessed with a permanent abode and a grove, he still felt the call of the desert as all bedouins were wont to. His heart occasionally still yearned to give up all material possessions and wander around the desert in the company of his sheep and camels, and lead an unfettered existence in its loneliness and fearlessness, just like his forefathers had before him. He often envied the free life his horse must have enjoyed in the desert before being captured and tamed by man.

A little while after he had reached home, he heard frantic shouting by an *asmar* (Black) servant who was employed in the palm grove. It was Bilal's brother.

Saqr ibn Shuja ibn Marri al-Sodari rushed out to investigate.

The retainer, who had served their family for generations, Bilal's brother, Musafir, who was crying bitterly, came running, shouting urgently, "*Abu* Ahmed....*ta'al*....*ta'al*...."

Saqr ibn Shuja ibn Marri al-Sodari remounted his horse and spurred it.

The horse galloped towards the palmgrove.

Upon reaching there, when he saw that all the newly planted saplings had been violently uprooted, he grew incandescent with rage and called out fiercely, "Bilal....Bilal...."

The black slave, Bilal lay bleeding on the ground stabbed to death. His dark body glinted in the sunlight.

Musafir yelled out, "Al-Mulaqim....It was Feda ibn Hammaad al-Mulaqim al-Sodari...."

Saqr ibn Shuja ibn Marri al-Sodari turned his horse around savagely. It began racing towards the settlement of the al-Mulaqims. Even though the al-Mulaqim and al-Zoubi were fraternal clans, there was no love lost between them. Their sworn enmity had a long tale behind it.

To find out the details of what sparked off their blood feud we need to go back to the time of Shuja ibn Marri ibn Sodari ibn Naqal ibn Deeb ibn Hrar ibn Jassas ibn Murra ibn Qulaif ibn Taqlib ar Rabiya, the father of the great-great-great-grandfather of the protagonist of this Chapter, Saqr ibn Shuja ibn Marri al-Zoubi al-Sodari.

It was the time when the *bedus* had come into Islam's fold for the second time.

Shuja ibn Marri ibn Sodari al Taqlib had arranged for a grand feast at his place that day. All the bedouins in the town had been invited to attend. The household of Shuja ibn Marri ibn Sodari al Taqlib was known to adhere strictly to all the tenets of Islam. The reason for his hosting the feast was to ensure that all the *bedus* in the region came together to also rigorously uphold all principles of Islam.

Every *bedu* in the area had responded positively to Sheikh Shuja ibn Marri ibn Sodari al Taqlib's invitation and turned up at the Sheikh's residence accompanied by their children.

As the elders relaxed in the tent, the children were playing inside the house. Ahmed ibn Shuja, the sixth son of Shuja ibn Marri ibn Sodari al Taqlib's second wife, was playing with a child belonging to the fraternal Bal-Al Hussein clan. Both were about the same age.

Amidst the din of the men's conversation inside the tent, Shuja ibn Marri ibn Sodari al Taqlib suddenly heard a shriek from his first wife, Noora bint Hammaad. Excusing himself, he went into the house to investigate. Just a few minutes ago he had been extolling the virtues of Islam, such as love, peace, brotherhood and universal amity to the bedus gathered at the tent.

As soon as he entered the house, he stood there stunned at the sight that met his eyes. His ten-year old son, Ahmed ibn Shuja had perpetrated an unimaginable act. He had decapitated the boy belonging to the Bal-Al Hussein clan like one would slaughter a goat. Shuja could hear the ladies of his household screaming in fright.

If this news reached outside, it would result in a huge clash. This was totally unacceptable behaviour at a banquet. The Bal-Al Hussein clansmen would now kill two men of the al-Zoubi clan in retaliation. It would then provoke the al-Zoubis to in turn slaughter four Bal-Al

Hussein men. And the cycle of violence would be set in motion once again. The blood-lust of the bedouins would never be satiated. When will Islam's teachings of peace and love seep into their consciousness? What a catastrophe at a time when the *bedus* were about to accept Islam's ways and turn into peaceable people? *Ya Allah*....Shuja ibn Marri ibn Sodari al Taqlib shuddered with apprehension.

He stood there totally enmeshed in confusion.

Islam preaches the avoidance of violence, he thought. Our family is one which follows Islam's dictates faithfully in every respect. We do not engage in any controversies or invite any trouble. Our generation obeys every law laid down in Islam, and our religion states that killing another human being is a mortal sin.

However, according to the bedouins' unwritten rules, if a man kills another, he forfeits the lives of at least two from his own family. This rule varies from clan to clan. Some claim four and some even seven lives to avenge the death of one of their clansmen. It was considered their just due and no one can prevent them from claiming this right. Twice the measure in return for love, but five times for enmity, seemed to be the accepted rule.

The Bal-Al Hussein clan would seek two lives for the death of one of theirs. What can I do to prevent it? *Ya Allah*....

Without any further thought, Shuja ibn Marri ibn Sodari al Taqlib grabbed hold of his ten-year old son, unsheathed the *jambiya* at his waist and in one swoop slashed the boy's throat and cast his lifeless body aside. He then caught hold of another boy who was nearby and severed his throat as well.

Total bedlam....

The first persons to reach the scene from the tent outside were his own al-Zoubi tribesmen.

They stood staring at the scene in disbelief.

It then took several seconds for everyone to realise that the second boy whose throat Shuja ibn Marri had cut was not one of his own sons, but a child belonging to the al-Mulaqim *faqat* (clan).

There had always been an undercurrent of hostility between the al-Mulaqims and the al-Zoubis. Despite belonging to the same *kabeela* (tribe) the two *faqats* had been at loggerheads for generations. One purpose of the feast was also to smooth over the relations between the two subsects.

Fearing an intense backlash, the al-Zoubis quickly gathered up Shuja ibn Marri ibn Sodari al Taqlib and fled. Owing loyalty to their *sheikh* and his family, they felt their primary duty was to protect them at any cost.

Shuja ibn Marri ibn Sodari al Taqlib wept as he prayed....

I have committed a heinous sin....like everyone else, I have allowed myself to be ruled by typical bedouin emotions and relinquished the Islamic path....I need to be punished for this transgression....I should be judged according to Shariah....please, my friends, hand me over to a *qaadi* (judge).....listen to my plea....let the enmity end with me....

No one among the group was willing to listen to his plea. We wouldn't allow any senior member of our al-Zoubi *faqat* to die.....this was a mistake committed by a small child....we have ourselves offered up retribution....in the confusion, our *sheikh* killed a child belonging to the al-Mulaqim clan thinking it was one of his own sons....it was not a deliberate act.....he sacrificed his own son without a moment's thought in order to safeguard our clan's honour.....our foremost duty to this person, who acted instinctively to protect our clan, is to ensure that he does not come to any harm....also, we needed to teach a lesson to the al-Mulaqims for continuously speaking ill of our community....they make fun of us saying we are the descendants of a harlot that our great-great-grandfather had brought and married from some unknown land....let the war to totally decimate them commence.....let's slaughter them to the last man....

The al-Zoubi tribesmen forcibly took away Shuja ibn Marri ibn Sodari al Taqlib on horseback and disappeared into the desert like the wind.

But the al-Mulaqims were everywhere searching for the person who had killed a young boy belonging to their *faqat*. Their search wouldn't end until they had found the murderer and killed him themselves. It did not matter how long the search lasted, they needed to kill him in revenge. If he was untraceable, they had every right to kill his brothers instead. No one had the right or the authority to prevent this from happening. The first target was the killer; if they found him and put him to death, the matter was considered closed. If not, the vendetta would continue, for generations, if need be....

The al-Zoubi tribesmen safeguarded Shuja ibn Marri ibn Sodari al Taqlib in the desert for ten long years. However hard they searched, the al-Mulaqims could not locate his whereabouts. In their anger and frustration, they extracted their revenge by eliminating one of his brothers. Once this happened, the al-Zoubis brought him back to town. As the blood debt had been paid, Shuja ibn Marri ibn Sodari al Taqlib could now lead a peaceful life. Since the al-Mulaqims had already extracted their pound of flesh, they could not harm him, as that would go against the bedouin code. If they committed such an act, then ten lives from their *faqat* would be forfeit. He could therefore breathe easy....

Shuja ibn Marri ibn Sodari al Taqlib lived peacefully till age 100, surrounded by his wives and grandchildren, and died of natural causes.

But the enmity between the al-Zoubis and the al-Mulaqims did not abate. There were constant minor irritations in their relationship. The vow of the al-Zoubis to completely eradicate the al-Mulaqim tribe remained only an empty threat.

The killing of the black retainer Bilal, belonging to the protagonist of this Chapter, Saqr ibn Shuja ibn Marri al-Zoubi al-Sodari, was part of a cycle of provocative acts that both sides indulged in.

Saqr ibn Shuja ibn Marri al-Sodari rode straight to the residence of Feda ibn Hammaad al-Mulaqim al-Sodari, dismounted, entered the house and shot Feda ibn Hammaad four times, killing him instantaneously.

A dispute regarding water sharing was behind the killing of the black slave, Bilal, by Feda ibn Hammaad al-Mulaqim al-Sodari. It was the practice of landowners to draw water for their *mazras* from a reservoir created by a check dam at the foothills of the desert mountains. The water was also used in summer for drinking purposes as well as to slake the thirst of their camels, apart from irrigating their fields. A system had been set up whereby the water was shared equitably. By that method, Saqr ibn Shuja al-Sodari was third in line to receive his supply of water. Disputing this age-old system, Feda ibn Hammaad al-Mulaqim al-Sodari's men had kicked up a row and, in the process, killed Saqr ibn Shuja's black slave, Bilal. But that alone could not be cited as the only reason.

The bedouin code did not permit the killing of slaves during hostilities between the different *faqats* in a *kabeela.* If such an event did take place, then the rules specified that only a slave belonging to the offending *faqat* should be killed in retaliation. This was one of the unwritten laws among the bedouins. But in violation of this code, Saqr ibn Shuja ibn Marri al-Sodari had shot dead the *bedu* who had killed his slave.

He had a strong motive behind his action. Saqr ibn Shuja ibn Marri al-Sodari considered Bilal his kinsman. It was a well-known fact that the black slave's great-great-grandmother had suckled his grandfather and in the process saved his life at birth. Bedouins put a lot of store by purity of blood. They would not even enter into marriage alliances with non-bedouin Arabs. If, however, for any reason a bedouin child had to be breastfed by a non-bedouin woman, her family members would be treated as kinfolk and accorded respect as such. Following this convention, since Saqr ibn Shuja ibn Marri al-Sodari's grandfather had drunk the milk of the black slave Bilal's great-great-grandmother, Bilal was considered a relative.

Saqr ibn Shuja ibn Marri ibn Saqr al-Zoubi al-Sodari sat in his *majlis* (meeting place) surrounded by the elders of the al-Zoubi *faqat*. As he sat with his head held high and looked around at the assembly, he could sense that the general feeling of the council was that he had committed an ill-judged act.

After a few moments' silence, Abdullah ibn Ahmed ibn Falah al-Zoubi al-Sodari, an elder of the al-Zoubi *faqat* and an adviser to Saqr ibn Shuja al-Zoubi al-Sodari, looked at him and gently broached the subject, "When they killed one of your black retainers shouldn't you have retaliated by killing one of their slaves in return? Why did you act like this? Does it behove a *sheikh* to breach our own canons?"

"They didn't kill a mere slave and you know it," replied Saqr ibn Shuja ibn Marri ibn Saqr al-Sodari heatedly.

"We do know that, but still....?" So saying, Abdullah ibn Ahmed ibn Falah al-Zoubi al-Sodari fixed his stare at Saqr.

"What are you saying, *Abu* Muhammad? Killing Bilal is equivalent to killing our grandfather...."

"I understand your feelings. What you did was fair, but leaving that aside for a moment, don't you see *Abu* Marri all your good intentions of following Islam's path of peace and avoidance of violence have been cast to the winds?"

Saqr ibn Shuja al-Zoubi al-Sodari lowered his eyes to the ground.

"Whatever your justification, what you did was wrong, " went on Abdullah ibn Ahmed relentlessly.

"Right or wrong, it is our duty to safeguard our *sheikh*," declared another al-Zoubi elder firmly.

"Are you saying that we should allow the person who came into our field and uprooted all our saplings to get away scot free, *Abu* Muhammad?" enquired a hothead in the council.

At this, Abdullah ibn Ahmed angrily remarked, "Sit down and keep quiet while the elders discuss this matter," and followed it up with some religious phrases.

Saqr ibn Shuja al-Zoubi al-Sodari looked at him and asked, "What's wrong with their questions, *Abu* Muhammad? How could he trespass into our land and pull out every sapling that we had planted?"

"I accept that was wrong, *Abu* Marri. But you, as a mature leader, should have acted in a more level-headed manner. Don't forget you are the *sheikh* of our *faqat*. Whenever such incidents have taken place earlier, we have always discussed the matter in our council and found a solution to the problem. Shouldn't you have thought with a clearer head instead of losing it altogether?" Abdullah ibn Ahmed tried to calm matters down. But Saqr ibn Shuja pounced on him instead.

"What are you saying *Abu* Muhammad? They committed two unpardonable wrongs…."

"What two wrongs? They killed a black slave whose ancestor suckled your grandfather and saved his life…. What's the other?" This question from Abdullah ibn Ahmed piqued the curiosity of everybody there.

In a low tone, Saqr ibn Shuja asked, "Should we then simply condone their trespassing into our land and uprooting our date saplings?" trying to divert the issue.

"We could have retaliated and called for a council meeting to sort out the issue. This does not warrant killing one of them. You are of course aware that the al-Mulaqims are growing in influence and are quite close to several emirs...." Abdullah ibn Ahmed sounded a note of caution.

"So what....?" retorted Saqr ibn Shuja angrily.

"What do you mean 'so what'?" responded Abdullah ibn Ahmed equally angrily. Saqr ibn Shuja detected a mocking tone in the question and his blood suddenly boiled at the slight.

"What are you talking about, *Abu* Muhammad? Do you want us to sit back and quietly watch them insult us by pulling up our palm saplings, and then suffer insult over injury at the council?"

"How is it an insult if palm saplings are uprooted?" Abdullah ibn Ahmed asked laughingly.

"That's precisely why they did that," Saqr ibn Shuja's fingers started to tremble.

"How do you see that, *Abu* Marri?" asked Abdullah as he gave a lopsided smile. Saqr ibn Shuja's heart began to pound harder when he saw that smile.

"I'm telling you that their intention was to humiliate us. Are you even listening to me?" As he said these words, Saqr ibn Shuja's head began to reel and his eyesight became blurred. Abdullah ibn Ahmed was senior to him by age, and bedouins were not in the habit of talking back to their elders. So, however hard Saqr ibn Shuja tried to temper his speech, he could not succeed. It seemed like Abdullah ibn Ahmed was siding with the al-Mulaqims who had tried to dishonour his *faqat*, and that feeling further enraged him. But Abdullah did not back down either and asked, "I don't follow you, *Abu* Marri....how is pulling up our saplings meant to humiliate us?"

"Yes, indeed....those were saplings from the date palms that our fathers and forefathers used to worship. The al-Mulaqims carried out their vandalism being fully aware of this fact. And you expect us to keep quiet about it? I say they pulled up all the saplings with the intention of slighting our fathers and forefathers." However hard he tried, he could not contain the explosion. Saqr ibn Shuja's entire body was now trembling with suppressed rage. How he wished he could kill the old man in front of him first before starting on the al-Mulaqims!

Upon hearing these words, a shocked Abdullah ibn Ahmed muttered, "La Illaha Il Allah….I can't believe what I'm hearing *Abu* Marri…. aren't you the one who keeps saying that there's no God but the all-knowing Allah, and strictly adhering to the path of Islam? You have even fought several battles to establish that principle….what are you now saying? I assert there is no god but Allah…."

Saqr ibn Shuja ibn Marri ibn Saqr al-Sodari stood rooted to the spot, utterly disconcerted.

Suddenly, a man came running, urgently yelling, "Let's get *Abu* Marri away from here….the al-Mulaqims are coming here with a big force…. hurry…get him away quickly…" and, in his headlong rush, stumbled and fell on Abdullah ibn Ahmed ibn Falah al-Sodari.

A horse could be heard neighing outside.

8

Sundar kept yelling and threatening, while Palani retained his calm. Rajendran looked at Palani and asked him, "What was I supposed to do when that Arab insisted I should go along with him? He got off at Tamra and asked me to bring his SUV back to the garage. How could I have refused him?" Having addressed the query to Palani, he glanced at Sundar's face which was flaming red with anger.

Palani smiled at Rajendran and commented, "You've got guts, I'll give you that....you travelled with a person who'd accused you of stealing his bag...."

Unblinking, Palani stared at Rajendran and continued, "You know he's a *bedu*, right? They're unstable fellows at the best of times.....I'm surprised he let you off so easily....weren't you even a little bit scared?" he asked, and eagerly awaited a reply, in an attempt to add to his knowledge of Arabian lore.

"Why should I be scared when I haven't stolen anything?" This short reply appeared to deflate Palani whereas it only seemed to infuriate Sundar further.

"Listen to the arrogant fellow *anna*....I'm sure he has filled the Arab's ears with lies about me....." he finally touched upon the point that was exercising his mind the most.

"Did you complain to him about your cousin, Rajendra?" Palani asked, in an attempt to repay Sundar for the biriyani he had treated him at the Malayali *bufiya* (restaurant) that afternoon.

"Why would I do that?" Sundar detected a false note in Rajendran's response and immediately came back with, "Don't believe him, Palani *anna*.....I know this fellow well.....I'm sure he must have said something....we should not let him off so easily....watch what I do to you....wait till I'm done with you," as he ranted and screamed in anger, spittle from his mouth sprayed onto Palani's *dhoti*. Suppressing his laughter, Rajendran responded equally angrily, "Look here....if you go on like this, I swear I won't be responsible for the consequences....."

Sundar's legs twitched in a futile attempt to kick at Rajendran. Palani prevented him from doing so. Failing in his effort to physically hurt him, Sundar vented his frustration by shouting at the top of his voice until his throat ran dry. "It's five thousand riyals....no small amount *anna*....if I don't get it back by tomorrow evening, I won't be responsible for the consequences...."

"Upon God I swear I didn't take the money Palani *anna*," responded Rajendran and glanced sideways at Sundar. Unable to sort out this matter, Palani threw in the towel, and saying, "Go to hell both of you....I'm done here. Sundara, do one thing, send him back to India and sort out your differences there....I'm out of here...." he got up to leave.

Sundar followed him saying, "Three thousand riyals have gone missing from that laundryman Ahmad's room also.....this fellow must have pinched that too...."

"Sundar *anna*, stop spreading false rumours about me....it won't do you any good...." Rajendran's eyes were fixed firmly upon Sundar.

Rajendran's words began to circle inside the room.

The sound of the door being locked echoed in his ears. He lay down on the floor. Unsure of what to do next, he fished out his mobile and telephoned Ahmad *bhai*. He was in the habit of visiting Ahmad's laundry and chatting with him frequently.

"Hello, Ahmad *bhai*....hello!"

Why isn't he responding? Has Sundar filled his head with his lies already?

He began scrolling through the WhatsApp videos on his mobile. Then he recalled Sundar's warning and his heart began racing. He began searching for and deleting all the nude videos that were on it. As he contemplated deleting the mobile app Nilla, he felt a burp coming up. The Arab, Shuja appeared in his mind's eye.

The Arab had told him to approach him if there was ever any problem.... he said he'd provide him a visa....I could go back to India and return on his visa.....

A sense of relief filled him, and sleep overcame him of its own volition.

The mobile was ringing. Rajendran snapped awake and picked it up. There had been ten missed calls. He checked the identity of the callers. His father had called him seven times on the Emo mobile app. The other three were from Ahmad *bhai.*

He called his father back.

His mother started crying at the sound of his voice. He just could not bear to hear her cry or the words she uttered.

"What's this I hear, Rajendra? Apparently you have stolen money from Sundar *anna*'s boss...they also say you've connections with illicit liquor distillers? And here I thought you'd turn over a new leaf and behave yourself in a foreign country.....but the reports about you are not all that good....I hear the punishment for wrong-doers in that country is beheading or amputation of hands or legs and deportation....why do you want to get involved in all this, my son? Your father was very adamant and was dead set against our only son going abroad....but

I didn't listen to him….I thought you'd do well as that country does not have liquor and the police is very strict with law-breakers….now I see I made a mistake in sending you there…..if something goes wrong, how do I answer your father? I swear I'll commit suicide…. if you have stolen the money, please fall at their feet, apologise and return it to them….please do not label us in the town as the parents of a thief….we've suffered enough as it is….What? Why don't you say something? Are you there? Hullo….hullo…."

Rajendran felt feverish. The image of the Bihari Mehboob Khan, which had been buried deep within his subconscious, suddenly rose before his eyes and shocked him. Fear again overwhelmed him.

Ahmad *bhai* also ranted furiously over the phone. He angrily vowed to go to the police unless the money was returned by the next day.

It seems I'm in cahoots with some Malayalis to distil illicit liquor….I also supposedly send x-rated videos over WhatsApp….I'm also in talks with a few Pakistanis to begin my own marijuana business…. the Saudi police are hot on my trail and is likely to arrest me at any moment….if the crimes are established, I'm sure to be beheaded…. Sundar is apparently going to the police with proof….

His heart beat so hard it almost shattered.

If I could return the money, everything would be sorted….what to do….how…..

If I did that, I would be branded a thief till his death….my actions would cause severe indignity to my parents….

Should I run away from this place, as I did in my dream? Or, should I seek refuge with the Arab? He's one person who would face any challenge unfazed, and will surely teach Sundar a proper lesson…. oh God, what am I to do….?

9

Fahad ibn Marra ibn Sodari ibn Naql ibn Deeb Banu al-Taqlib declaimed his verses at the top of his voice.

The wind in the valley was caressing the shadows of the *gustal* trees. That is where Fahad ibn Marra was belting out his compositions in the presence of a fellow poet. Even though this desert valley was called Wadi al Daqeen, Fahad had instinctively realised that this was the fabled *Abqer Wadi,* the place frequented by *jinns.* He had reached the cradle of poetry, a place which was out of bounds to hundreds of bedouin poets. As soon as he figured out that he had arrived at *Abqer Wadi,* he yelled out in exultation, and began to recite his poem out loud. Apart from his fellow poet, there were no other human beings around to share in his jubilation.

Perhaps because of the towering mountains surrounding it, or its remote location, or the fear of *jinns* that populated it, not many dared to come here. A small, almost hidden, perennial pond brimmed with water all year round. Fahad, Sodari's grandson, having followed the trail of the untamed desert wind, negotiated the tall mountains and discovered that legendary valley with the *gustal* trees, had hugged and kissed his compatriot, and loudly proclaimed, "*Abqer Wadi, ya rajjaal.....adhi Abqer Wadi*!"

As soon as he paid obeisance to the *gustal* trees and spied the *jinns* inhabiting them, the lines automatically took shape in his mind:

Having made my life's path smooth,
And brought me to your land
As a poet and seer, Oh, jinn of my heart,
You've made my life pleasurable.

My dreams
Dance before my eyes.
Bring forth all your companions
And steep me in your fragrant perfume.

I float in the air;
Here are thousands of jinns
Loving beings that bathe my body
In a pool of fire.

My dear friend,
Declare loudly, let all the poets hear.
Sing loudly about my kinship
With the jinns of Abqer Wadi.

On the third day of the waning moon,
Fix your sight on the Tamar star that appears in the North
Then travel eastward until the Elephant star is directly ahead.
That's when this alternative universe will appear straight ahead.
It's no easy task to reach this magical land.

Keep swimming in the summer air,
You'll be drawn here one fine evening.
You'll then drown in Abqer Wadi's magic.
Until then keep suckling on the milk of the sands,

And engaging in coitus with the stars.

Here's the source of all poetry,
I'm at the colourful world of jinns
Singing my compositions,
Proud that a jinn just like you
Is inside of me.

Cavorting gleefully and shouting out the lines with great enthusiasm, Fahad ibn Marra ibn Sodari celebrated *Abqer Wadi* in the company of the *jinns* present there.

Even though he had begun by singing the glories of his *faqat* (clan), as per his grandfather's wishes, those memories had faded from his consciousness long back. Time, lust, flora, stars, rain, blazing desert winds, freezing winter nights and human emotions now dominated his compositions. The *jinns* presented him with a special falcon fledgling they brought from somewhere. He trained it to become a keen hunter. It would fly faster than the wind, hunt small birds and bring the kills back to Fahad ibn Marra with lightning speed. *Jinns* would appear before his eyes at the time when the plumage of bird turned golden in the firelight of kindling set ablaze by the sparking of flints. They would heap praise upon Fahad ibn Marra, the *kahin* (poet and seer), calling him the handsomest man in the world of *jinns,* and help him create newer and better verses. He would absorb the scent of that ethereal world through his eyes and, holding his breath for a short while, allow himself to drown in the effervescence of the sparks. He would take a deep draught of the wine offered by his companion, and sing his compositions out loud.

It was while he was declaiming his verses that day that he spotted an unfamiliar *jinn* floating in midair. He stopped and wonderingly asked, "I have never seen you before in *Abqer Wadi*....Who are you? I was told there was just one *jinn* world. Where are the rest of the *jinns*? I don't see any of them around...." He got up and looked around him for the other *jinns*. But not one was visible. His poet-friend was sleeping soundly nearby.

Hovering upside down in midair, the *jinn* gave a loud laugh and replied, "I too belong to this world. I used to reside in a man such as yourself. He was also a great connoisseur and loved poetry dearly. That is why I entered him and enabled him to compose many poems for the pleasure of mankind. But, times have changed, my friend.... humankind does not respect poetry any longer. A poet is looked upon with suspicion these days. There was a time when poets were regarded with admiration and respect....and we used to bask in that admiration vicariously, knowing it was directed at us. And we limned with our words a world that was beyond the ken of ordinary folk. We depicted human history going back generations by describing the lives of your forefathers. But, today, no one has any need for it. The world around us has changed, my friend....words such as God, angels, nymphs, heaven and hell are once again being employed. These will annihilate not just us, but destroy all human spirit and capabilities as well. Cognizant persons such as yourself are a dwindling minority....and might one day become totally extinct....that's my biggest worry ...." With these introductory words, the *jinn* descended and sat down in front of him.

Fahad ibn Marra gazed keenly at the *jinn* that glided down as gracefully as a waterfall flowing downhill. It was a bewitching female *jinn*. His heart leaped. He wished he could hug her and plant a kiss on her lovely face. He suppressed that urge and said in a shocked tone, "You're uttering words I've never heard before.....they're words that our humankind have never used before....what kind of places are heaven and hell? I don't understand at all....I've heard of words like angels, nymphs and god.... I also know that some *bedus* belonging to western Arabia use the word 'God', but this is the first time I hear of the other terms ...."

"Yes, my friend....humankind is undergoing a transformation at this moment....till now, an alternative universe to you meant our universe, and humans pictured the existence of us *jinns* through the words of *kahins* such as yourself....they attempted to visualise the existence of unseen images and objects, and grasp the volatile moments present in the theory of time continuum, comprising elements such as yesterday, today and tomorrow, through your words....But, unfortunately, they have once again reverted the thousands-of-year-old outdated, artificial concepts such as god, heaven and hell, and regressed to antiquated practices. All this while, for the majority of men, there was nothing other than the world that existed right in front of their eyes. *Kahins* such as yourself are an exception to this rule. That is why people like you are considered eccentric by the rest of mankind. Forget it, that's a topic for another day....but they do appreciate and enjoy your poems and conjectures about the future of the world, don't they? They led their life happily in the thought that the beauty of life does not lie in either yesterday or tomorrow, but in the moments I perceive now, right in front of my eyes. You are people who lead their lives according to the hedonistic philosophy propounded by Aristippus of Greece. But, once the doctrines of Socrates and Plato began to rule this world again, you quit your motherland, Cyrene, and made your way towards Damascus. Later you abandoned that too and, eschewing transformations, you returned to the previous world of wonders. I readily admit we grew jealous of your lifestyle of 'wine, women and song' after you had come to the realisation that this life and how we live it is what we make of it ourselves. However, your kind has again begun to transform itself, my friend.....the old world order has slowly started to dominate once again. As a result, I fear that *kahins* such as yourself, who imbue us with life, would soon be extinct."

The *jinn* then embraced Fahad ibn Marra and planted a kiss on the crown of his head as though saluting his extraordinary brain.

He could make no sense of what the *jinn* was talking about. Greece and Plato were just words to him. He however enjoyed listening to the knowledgeable voice of the *jinn*. Like a fiery waterfall, the words made his body burn and he attempted to hug the intelligent being tightly and press its breasts against his chest. While he managed to get his arms around it, the *jinn*'s body never touched his own. Spreading his legs wide, he tried to place it on his lap and plant a kiss on its lips. The *jinn* slid smoothly out of his grasp, once again suspended itself upside down in midair and laughing loudly exclaimed, "Hahaha.... you restless human....your male sexism is showing....did you think you could have sex with a *jinn* and create history of sorts? Hahaha.... although you can see my breasts, you cannot fondle them....hahaha.... remember one thing, though.....unless you make philosophies your life, hedonism may disappear from this world forever ...." Saying this, the *jinn* took flight and disappeared from sight.

As soon as the *jinn* vanished into thin air, the other *jinns,* which had gone underground, came out of their hiding places and said, "Whew, at last she's gone....her words are enough to make one's head whirl....that's why, as soon as we smell her coming, we run and hide underground.....you were unlucky enough to be her scapegoat today....hahaha....what was she on about all this while?"

The *jinns* went on speaking. As twilight began to fall, Fahad paid close heed to their words hoping to unlock life's mysteries and secrets. Human world, the world of *jinns*. Desert, heat, cold, fire, blood, human form, *jinns*' souls, formless lust, insensate body, living desert, poetry- spouting humans, imaginings of real versus artificial, fervour for home and country, the wind that oscillates between light and darkness, the ever-beating pulse, the occasional human tumescence.... all these topics continued after pauses for deep breaths in between.

Fahad ibn Marra ibn Sodari al Taqlib stood there in stunned silence. Oblivious of his state, the *jinns* continued:

There are two groups within us. One resides with humans while the other stays back at *Abqer Wadi*. When the first group grows tired of living among human beings, they return to *Abqer Wadi* and relate stories of the other world to the rest of us. When they hear these tales, the *jinns* from the homeland fly towards the human world to continue their contribution towards poetry. Each returning *jinn* selects one of us as an extension of themselves. But the catch lies in the fact that on no account would they reveal the details of the person they were in possession of in the human world. They would simply relate tales of that person's ancestors and go underground to hibernate. The *jinns* from here would use their poems as clues to try and track down the individual concerned. This is an ancient game among us. If any *jinn* loses the game, by our rules, it should not enter a human body for three years and must spend that time suspended in midair. A year in our calendar is equal to ten moonless days, or five months by your almanac. Entering a person's consciousness is a celebration of sorts for us. You and your world consist of hundreds of sensations that are not present in ours. For example, our universe does not consist of emotional trips involving tears, laughter or amazement. In our immortal existence, the moment humans turn to dust again is a very special instant. Moving around using a human's arms and legs for locomotion, composing poetry after having taken possession of their minds, absorbing wine into our souls, providing them enjoyment by aiding their love-making with the opposite sex for hours on end.... Wow....that's something else! It's an experience like no other....it's a gratifying world where we wish our imperishable existence would come to a peaceful end whilst in that corporeal body.

We too engage in sexual relations, *kahin*. When we return from your world to ours, we engage in copulation. Laughing at man's puny five minutes' effort, we lock our sexual organs and go underground while engaging in congress for four full moons. We rejuvenate your roots there and make them sprout. When the fresh shoots germinate, we absorb the intoxicating drops from your roots and, emerging from the soil, engage in fresh sexual relations with yet another *jinn*. You need to watch our sex act at least once in your lifetime. No other being in this world is capable of our sexual feats. Oh….I forgot to mention something….apart from human beings, we also occasionally enter the bodies of animals….but to us a human body is preferable, because only they can compose poetry like us….but, when we spot anyone trying to organise their lives as elegantly as poetry, we grow angry and enter their bodies just so we can disrupt their efforts to coordinate and regulate their lives.

But we do not enter just anybody's body freely and easily. We only select those who respect us or those who welcome our presence. We do not approach those who detest or disrespect us. However poetic their souls might be, if they do not like us, we would not even go near them. We select only those poetic souls who have been rejected by their fellow-humans. We would be a source of constant strength in their life's journeys. We would fortify their hearts and strengthen their resolve to live. We would make them realise that life is meant for living. Since death is a certainty, we would urge them to live their lives according to their desires.

As Fahad went on listening to these accounts, he recalled a snippet from a *jinn* that had come from elsewhere and, one morning, he scaled the mountains, crossed *Abqer Wadi* and plunged into the desert beyond it. He started walking towards the horizon. Memories of his friends and relatives began to blossom in his mind. A battalion of *jinns* followed in his wake. Every time he grew tired, one of them would enter into him, provide him with fresh poetry and revitalise him.

Fahad ibn Marra ibn Sodari paused for a moment, closed his eyes and, as though coming to a realisation, began to run wildly with his eyes still shut. The entire desert along with the *jinns* started running after him. As he ran, he began shouting, "I need to save my *faqat* and my *kabeela.....thaqfa....thaqfa....*" He somehow finally managed to reach the men belonging to his *faqat.*

When the men, who were resting under a shady tree, saw him come rushing, they stood up in shock and welcomed him, saying, "*Arhab* (welcome), *ya kahin.....arhab....*" He acknowledged their welcome with the words, *Al bega, al bega....*", recited a poem in response and then burst out, "My kinsmen, you're all in mortal danger....I've been entrusted with the responsibility of saving my kind....come with me to *Abqer Wadi* where the *jinns* reside....our entire clan is in danger of being annihilated....trust me, as your *kahin,* I'm able to foresee the coming danger...."

He was given a drink from a camel-skin water bag and some dates to eat. Surprisingly the *sheikh* was present there along with the *gazu. Gazu* refers to a bedouin army whose sole mission is to annihilate enemy *kabeelas* or combatant members of sub-sects belonging to the same *faqat.* All male members of the *kabeela* had gone with them to raid an enemy camp and were relaxing there after their successful foray. The *sheikh* came forward and, after inviting Fahad ibn Murra to sit on a sand dune, began talking to him.

"Our *gazu* is returning after laying waste to the camp of our *kabeela*'s archenemy. Our entire *kabeela* had gone along with them on the raid after gaining a solemn promise that this would be their last act of violence. We're about to return to the religious path that we had abandoned previously. That renunciation had commenced at the time you were still here among us....remember? Some demanded that we forswear our ancestors' methods of worship and follow the path shown by the Prophet (Peace Be Upon Him), while others resisted that demand. There are some among us who still claim that we should not abandon the ways of our ancestors. You are a *kahin.* Our *kahin,* who is able to see the future and express it in verse form. In order to walk the straight path shown by the almighty, we need to eschew violence, drink and debauchery and once again adopt the religious ways that we had previously cast by the wayside. This is the best method by which every bedouin clan can become united and worship the One God. Some among us still resist this move. You're a clever man and have a way with words. Tell them in a poetic form and make them understand.....come....we need to walk the spiritual path shown to us by the Prophet (PBUH)....that doesn't mean we need to entirely abandon the ways of our ancestors....all we need to do is make some changes in the God we worship and our ways of life, that's all....our people need to learn to read and write....they need to be able to read the holy book and steer our life onto the right path....do you understand?" Fahad ibn Marra ibn Sodari sat there with his head bowed.

He looked around. The *jinns* that had accompanied him stared into his eyes. The *jinn* inside him, anguished at being unable to compose poetry any longer, slid out of his body and went to join its compatriots.

Fahad ibn Marra ibn Sodari lifted his head and gazed around. A large group of horsemen were seen galloping towards them. The entire clan stood up in shock. The *gazu* quickly gathered up their swords, daggers, bows and arrows and stood ready on their heels to repel any attack.

The horsemen proceeded directly towards them. What followed next was anticlimactic for the *gazu* which awaited their *sheikh*'s order to repel the perceived attack.

The pack of horsemen were a troop of *Aquaon* (a religious group) returning from a victorious campaign in Baghdad. Some, who could not bear to see their *sheikh* conversing with them cordially, let out shouts of dissent. The *sheikh* chided them and, turning to Fahad ibn Marra ibn Sodari, said by way of introduction, "This is the group I was telling you about. He is the person who is guiding us onto the Almighty's path." He then turned to the bearded man seated on his horse and said, "Sir, this is our *kahin*."

The horseman nodded his head and said gravely, "No more *kahin*, *jinn* or poetry. We'll finish you off if there is any more violence or wine and women. We are returning from Baghdad after slaughtering those who were deviating from the true path. If anyone here talks of Bedouin gods, ancestral practices and suchlike, they would face the same fate as the Baghdadis, am I clear? There is only one God in this entire universe. And we should lead our lives as prescribed in the holy book. The punishment for any barbaric practice like female infanticide or eulogising harlots is death, understood? I'll shortly be deputing someone to visit your *kabeela* and train you in the proper religious practices....and, you, poet, stop spreading lies like 'I've a *jinn* inside of me, I can foresee tomorrow's events today' and such-like, got it?"

Fahad ibn Marra ibn Sodari looked him in the eye, laughed, and replied, "Look behind me...there's a whole group of *jinns* standing right here....you dare make fun of *kahins*? One word from me is enough to make you all turn tail and run for your lives....do you want a demonstration?" He slapped his thigh in challenge.

His *sheikh* came quickly forward, shoved him aside and urgently said, "Get away, you *majnun* ....*Ya rajjaal*, someone get him away from here quickly...."

The bearded elder drew his sword, jumped off his horse in one smooth motion, stood for a moment staring unblinkingly at Fahad ibn Marra ibn Sodari, and then walked up to him.

Fahad ibn Marra, the *kahin*, the poet and seer, stood there glaring at him defiantly.

The elder pointed his sword at Fahad's face and shouted furiously, "Summon your *jinns*....call them, *ya shaitan*...." He was fit to burst.

Fahad ibn Marra laughed out loud and started to recite a poem....

Before he could finish the first line, a jet of blood spurted out of his neck and his head rolled on the ground. With open eyes, his head stared fixedly straight ahead as it lay still on the desert sand.

Holding his blood-stained sword aloft, the elder loudly proclaimed, "There is no god but Allah!" All his followers unsheathed their swords and repeated his declaration of faith.

The Banu Murra bedouins of the Sodari tribe looked on with shock at the lifeless body of their *kahin* lying unclaimed on the ground. At the sound of the swords being drawn and the fervent chanting by the *aquaon* they turned around in stupefaction.

The elder's speech now turned into a sermon:

"No more talk of *kahins*, divination and poetry….anyone believing the word of a deranged person henceforth will also be suitably punished…. our holy book has detailed every event that is likely to take place as long as human race exists….that is God's true path and that is the righteous and true direction….that is the word of the omniscient god….you must henceforth live by the law and moral guidance laid down in another book that derives scriptural authority from the holy book….only by following those rules can you hope to achieve *jannah* (heaven)....some of you still worship trees, don't you? My men will chop down those trees. Let me see if your god comes to your rescue. God is formless, but all-powerful and all-knowing…. fools….he activates the entire universe and is not visible to human eyes….your barbaric worship methods must cease with immediate effect….from now on, it's one god and one religion only….all your previous practices such as violence, illicit sexual relationships, liquor drinking, theft, idol worship will be eradicated from today….anyone who violates these rules will be severely punished…." He then turned to the group of Black retainers who stood there cringing servilely and roared out, "From now on no one is anyone's slave, we're all of us the Almighty's slaves, is it understood?"

10

Rajendran lay on his bed, cross-legged, staring at the ceiling. As he considered ways and means of extricating himself from the web Sundar was weaving around him, his thoughts suddenly veered towards the more pleasant images of the scantily-clad seductresses who featured in his mobile app Nilla. The worm inside his underpants stirred as he imagined them removing their scanty garments and posing naked for his titillation. He immediately experienced a hard-on.

He had come across the advertisement for Nilla while using his Emo mobile app for calling home, and had become immediately intrigued by it. He was however unsure whom he should consult about it. He had embraced Nilla wholeheartedly before becoming fearful that the presence of x-rated videos on his phone might attract severe punishment from the local police, and deleted them all. The app now beckoned him once again and gave him the necessary boost.

It was Hassan from Bangladesh who had led him into this magical world. Whenever Hassan visited his garage, he would whisper into Rajendran's ears the method to navigate the web and enter Nilla and other similar applications. He had shown Rajendran how to use a stream called CPN to enter this paradise of houris, and made Nilla Rajendran's palmtop gateway to heaven. If you showered sufficient gold coins upon the girls featured in Nilla, they would oblige you by taking off their clothes and displaying their natural charms for you to feast your eyes on. He would melt at the sight of hitherto unseen lady parts. He would shower kisses upon the mobile phone's screen while lying back delightedly. He would take screenshots of the lady bits and save them secretly on his phone. At times when he was broke, he would secretly view those visuals and masturbate.

He was initially scared that the local police might nab him for possession of pornography. But Hassan had encouraged him saying, "My friend, according to CPN, you're actually a resident of the United States. So, don't be afraid. No one can trace you....it's a secret server...." So saying, Hassan had led him to a wonderland where he splurged two and three hundred riyals every month to stare awestruck at forbidden pieces of female anatomy, touching them vicariously, getting aroused, and night after night converting cash into cum. He had also on occasions rued the fact that his much-needed money was turning into frothy spunk, but would then comfort himself with the thought that this was a more pleasurable way of wasting money than buying Thailand lottery tickets. He would spend such magical moments with the beauties from Nilla at least once a month. But every time he exited the application, his body and mind would experience a hollow feeling.

His heart would feel empty. There had also been nights when he had lain awake fearing that the sperm bank within his body had gone dry. He was dreaming of the day when he would win big in the Thailand lottery, construct a palace in his hometown, deck his mother out with gold ornaments, buy a car and employ a chauffeur for his father and get a BMW and a luxurious bungalow in the city for himself. He would sometimes feel troubled that these dreams were being thwarted by the sirens of Nilla.

Some nights, he would wake up suddenly in the middle of his sleep and come out for air. It was not just the "Nilla itch" that would cause this but also certain strange, recurrent dreams. Some very odd dreams....the police beheading him....his mother featuring on the Nilla app....the body of Singaram *mama*'s daughter but with the face of that Arab, Shuja, who seductively takes off her clothes and, fondling her breasts, invites Rajendran to make love to her. Rajendran nears Singaram *mama*'s daughter, who looks like Shuja, with the intention of having sex with her. Speaking in a feminine voice, Shuja caresses his breasts and takes off his panties. He kneels before Shuja, who has the torso of Singaram *mama*'s daughter, and starts sucking Shuja's dick. As he raises his head to look up, Shuja slashes his throat with his *jambiya* (dagger). When such troubling dreams bother him, he would suddenly wake up, look around him in confusion and would shiver in fear, scared to stay in his room. He would then get up and walk out. His heart would experience a slight empty feeling then.

He would grow annoyed that he had come to a foreign country only to suffer in silence in this manner.

That pain would drag him back to his hometown and to his family and make him suffer untold agonies.

In the same manner, he was reminded of the loan his father had taken from Raghu *mama* and tormented him. He decided at that very moment.

Whatever happens, he would not leave this country until he had finished constructing a house back home and bought a car.....but.... what to do in the meantime? Should I return the money? After all, Sundar has already telephoned home and informed everybody....

Just wait, Sundar you scoundrel....I won't let you badmouth me in front of our families....I swear I'll change my name if I don't get back home and send you a video of me having sex with your wife....son of a bitch.....you think you can take me on....you made me suck your prick while I was a small boy .... wait till I get your wife to give me a blow job in return....

11

They joined forces to go to war within a year of Sodari ibn Naql ibn Deeb Banu Murra al Taqlib ar Rabiya's passing. Those were the days when the Banu Murra *kabeela* had still not parted ways with the main Taqlib group to form their own separate Sodari *kabeela*.

They were mounting an assault on Jebel Aflaj with a view to annihilating the Isbah *faqat*, kin to their grandfather's three brothers, who had attacked and ransacked the Sodari clansmen's dwellings. Their camel legion, accompanied by a few horses, kicked up a huge dust storm in its wake.

The war party consisted of both nomadic Sodaris and a group of settlers. They were also accompanied by a retinue of Black slaves. The town-dwelling Sodaris had somehow overcome the nomadic group's objection to involving the slaves in their fight, and succeeded in bringing them along. Some of the nomads had argued vehemently against the slaves' inclusion, stating that 'we are not cowards to make slaves fight our battles while we stand idly by and watch from far', 'our Taqlib *kabeela* is capable of fighting the very thunder and lightning in the skies'. and 'we are not like the cowardly Isbah *faqat* who need the backing of slaves to fight their battles'. A compromise that 'the slaves will not join in the fight until all of us agree' had finally been reached, and the force had set out. A few burly slaves were mounted on camels. Some clung on to the camels while several ran determinedly alongside the animals. Their musical instruments, such as the *Tablah* and the *Tar*, were attached with ropes to the underbellies of the camels allotted to them.

In the forefront of the force, brandishing their swords, in a frenzy of anticipation of the slaughter to come, were Sodari's sons and grandchildren, surrounded by the *faqat*'s warrior group known as the *gazu*. They were intent upon avenging the slur on their elder's name. A handful of Sodari women were also seen on the camels urging the mounts forward, while their brothers rode along with them.

This war had begun a year after Sodari's death and just before the wedding feast of the last son of his fifth wife drew to a close. It was the first wedding in the family after his demise. The festivities were being held under the stewardship of his eldest son. That is when the seeds of the war had been sown.

Following Sodari's passing, his first son had been expected to take over as the sheikh of their *faqat*. That was also the normal practice among the bedouins. But it was well-recognised among them that, beyond the fact that the first-born son had no inclination to assume the mantle, he lacked the competence to handle the role. He himself was fully aware of his shortcomings and so kept postponing his anointment as the sheikh. He kept mulling over the question as to who among his brothers was the best suited for the role. There had also been constant squabbles among them. Each was competent in his own right. But in his mind he had a nagging fear that his desire to name a competent person, who measured up to his father's stature, might culminate in a bloodbath. This apprehension kept him from announcing a final choice. There was also another reason for his confusion: left to himself, he would have preferred to roam freely in the desert rather than stay put in a settlement. It was while he was on the verge of naming one of his brothers as the sheikh, and merging himself with the unfettered wind in the desert, that the incident took place, leaving him with no option but to assume command of the war party.

One group of Sodari's sons still roamed the desert while another lot had settled down in fixed abodes. Among the Taqlibs, the Sodari's Banu Murra *kabeela* was growing in strength and influence in the Najd area of Eastern Arabia. By entering into marriage alliances with the *bedus* of the North and the West, they were emerging as the dominant *kabeela* in the Najd province. With the intention of carrying on the proud tradition of the Sodaris, and with a view to expanding their bloodline, each scion produced twenty to thirty offspring, thus establishing their numerical superiority as well. While some paid homage to their ancestor by naming the valley they lived in after him, the nomads among them did not abandon the desert and continued their itinerant lifestyle to keep his memory alive.

While both groups were united in their resolve to lay down their lives in defence of their *kabeela*, a few among them envied the other's way of life also. Some of the desert nomads craved the calm and peaceful life of their settled cousins while a few from the latter group were drawn inextricably by the magical pull of the desert. It was also not uncommon for the two opposite poles to occasionally meet and exchange places. There was no fixed rationalisation or time period for such exchanges. It was also one of the reasons why this war had commenced. The event that was the trigger had taken place while Sodari had been still alive, but it assumed a life of its own only towards the end of his son's marriage ceremony.

The wedding itself was over and arrangements for the night's revelry were proceeding apace. The atmosphere was warming up nicely with poetry, songs and dancing. The men were drinking wine and snacking on fruits prior to dinner. A few of them were adding intoxicating herbs to their wine in order to achieve a high, so that they may sing the poems generated by the *jinns* residing within them.

The Sodaris of the settlement, mindful that this was the very first wedding in the family after the passing of their elder, were keen on ensuring that all the arrangements were perfect so that their nomadic cousins may have no grounds for complaints regarding the hospitality extended to them.

As a prelude to the feast, the slaves were serving the assembled guests with tea, wine and fruits. A *fursha* (carpet) had been laid out in front of the *qasr* (house) and all the male guests were seated on it. The burning *samar* logs in the bonfire were spreading their fragrance everywhere. The men were using an incense-holder in which *misk* (secretions from the musk deer) and *oudh* (extract from the agar tree) from al-Hind (India) were smouldering in burning coals, to infuse their faces and bodies with the aromatic smoke, and passing it around among themselves. Some of them had *Rehan* (a fragrant leaf) tucked in their turbans and waistbands. Around them, lights in glass holders struggled to provide sufficient illumination.

The women were preparing the wedding feast in the house with assistance from the slaves. A few bedouin men were supervising the arrangements. Whole sheep were roasting in huge makeshift ovens, while rice from India was bubbling in cauldrons. Women of the desert, to whom rice was a novelty, were watching it boil with childlike curiosity. Others were busy preparing flatbreads known as *al Kurs* and *al Margooga* from flowers found in the desert, and piling them in serving dishes. Some women were cooking other dishes using corn and wheat. Sheep and a whole young camel were barbecuing on spits in the ground. Trays holding fruits and wine were being sent out in relays to the men outside. All this activity was creating wonder and excitement among some of the nomadic women. But it seemed to irk a few others who went around from group to group warning that our entire lineage would be destroyed if we became addicted to this decadent lifestyle. At least a dozen of the women were pregnant. They were being provided special attention and specific dishes were being prepared specially for their benefit. When they suddenly heard the men raise a shout, the women focussed their attention outside. Some ran out to view the scene from a distance. A few stood in front of the men and began dancing along with them. Singing a tune known as *al Khal Khaal*, the women provided an added impetus to the men's dancing.

A group of men were holding their swords and canes aloft and dancing. Some were firing arrows in the air and yelling. Everyone had leather belts around their waists in which *jambiyas* (daggers) nestled in their scabbards. They all had turbans wrapped around their heads. A few, seated on sand dunes, singing all forms of *qasidas* (poems) like *meshhoob*, *majroor* and *mankoos*. Their poems spoke of ancient wars fought by their ancestors, their victories in battles, the assistance they rendered to wayfarers, the thefts they committed, and their wanderings in the desert in the company of camel caravans.

Standing in two lines, facing each other, they were performing the *ardha* (a warrior folk dance). Stepping back and forth, shaking their swords up and down and occasionally singing counterpoint to the melody in progress they were paying respect and bidding adieu to the night. The women stood in a line, holding hands, and danced, gently swaying their bodies in sync with their feet.

The slaves stood to one side, watching their masters dancing and singing the *ardha*, and eagerly awaiting their turn on the dance floor. Some of them looked at each other as though silently mocking, 'what sort of celebration is this without musical accompaniments'?

The slaves' celebrations would begin after the bedus ended their poetry recitations and dancing. However not all of them would participate in the dancing. Only a few slaves would perform the *saamri* (folk dance) while the rest would continue to attend to their masters' needs. It was an unspoken rule that their performance would commence only after the bedus' *ardha* ended. But this time, when the bedus began to sing proudly about the accomplishments of their Sodari elder, the bodies of some black slaves became galvanised and began to twitch as the dancing *jinns* entered them. They stretched their arms out and began jumping up and down in a frenzy. When he saw this, an infuriated Bal Al, the son of Sodari's fourth wife, began to lay about the dancing Blacks with the flat of his sword. Some of the bedus intervened and pulled him away, among whom was Zoubi, the son of Sodari's fifth wife. After pulling his brother away, Zoubi angrily reminded the slaves that their turn to celebrate had not come yet. He then instructed that the wounded slave be taken to a well-lit spot and examined for injuries. A few slaves carried the wounded man away for a more thorough examination. At times like this, it was usual for everyone to look to Zoubi because of his good rapport with the slaves. After the elder Sodari, it was Zoubi whom the slaves respected the most. He was also the one who afforded them the utmost protection. It was Zoubi who made sure the slaves were properly fed and clothed, and given the occasional drink of wine. He also ensured they received proper medical attention when they were injured. A few of his brothers were against such mollycoddling, but, since everyone recalled that their father had himself tacitly sanctioned such acts, they held their peace.

Zoubi stood still, motionless. His eyes gravitated towards his pregnant fourth wife. She was in her full term. While she had two black women attending to her full-time, he was still feeling anxious.

Alongside her stood Zoubi's fifth wife. His glance fell on her. For some reason he was reminded of a rampant stallion mounting a mare. Her body attracted him like a magnet. He fretted that she was yet to become pregnant despite being married to him for eighteen months now. He felt that she cared more for him than his other four wives.

Once when he had developed a large and painful boil near his rectum, it was she who had caringly applied balm on it….'How much anguish she must have felt when I had kidnapped her from her settlement and brought her here by force ….?' 'Is she still pining for her parents back home and hurting inside….?'

Zoubi ibn Sodari had occasionally plumbed the depths of sorrow, a state of mind known as *Al Wenin* among the bedouins. He had also composed a poignant poem on her beauty.

Her lush tresses, that embellish the night,
Are like an oasis in the desert.
How do I express in words, my friend
The manner in which her eyes, that overwhelm the stars,
Weaken me and render me irresolute?
I cannot express in words
How her laughter captivates the very moon.

Even in your wildest dreams
You cannot imagine!
Her clothes cast off,
Hair blowing wildly in the wind….
Close your eyes and
Listen to my words….
Her breasts are like a
Newborn's head emerging from the womb.
Soft and spongy….
But, if I tell you they provide strength to my fingers,
You'll claim I'm probably fornicating with a jinn!

Have you heard of the banana?
It is a fruit from the land of the Blacks (Africa)
Her thighs are like the banana stalks

Between them lie honey bees waiting to ambush me.
The queen bee gets entangled with my tongue
And the entire pleasure grove erupts with rapture.
That's when the camel, with its hump cast off,
Stands erect as though challenging the very skies.
I cannot describe to you the feeling
Of samar trees drenched in rain, swallowing me whole
As though I'm drowning in a mist of opium.

If we had been in our great-grandfather's time,
I'd have let you savour the experience yourself.
Together we could have celebrated her
Like we played with ourselves in our youth,
We could have devoured her jointly....

Zoubi had composed this *qasida* and recited it to his brother and close confidant, Mulaqim.

This fifth wife of Zoubi was the root cause of the war that was now being waged against the Isbah *kabeela*. Even as those who were hoping for a conflict to erupt during the past one and a half years - ever since Zoubi ibn Sodari al Taqlib abducted and brought her here by force - were secretly gladdened by the declaration of war, the sole reason for this war, Zoubi's fifth wife, had fallen into a swoon when the war had broken out.

When Zoubi had brought her home that day on his camel, Sodari had erupted in delight and, slapping his right thigh in challenge and stroking his *shenab* (moustache), had proudly proclaimed, "*Akhu Noora*, let's see who comes to her rescue....escort her to the women's quarters....*ya walad*, where's that young *kahin*? Summon him.... ask him to sing.....let's hear how it happened...." Before he finished speaking, a figure pushed through the ranks of men in front of him and, planting a kiss on Sodari's forehead, stood before him with its head bowed down. Sodari boomed, "Lift your head up....what's his name? Who's his mother? I've forgotten," looking at the person in front of him, confused as to whether it was his fourth wife's fifth son or seventh. The boy looked up at his grandfather and introduced himself, "I'm Fahad bin Marra bin Sodari al Taqlib".

Sodari guffawed loudly and remarked, "Hmmm….I must be growing old…I can no longer tell my grandsons from sons ….So you're a *kahin* too, are you? I thought it was only my son from the woman from the East who composed poetry….you do too, eh? All right, go on….you were away for months on end….where did you all go? How did he abduct this girl from our enemy's *kabeela*? Have you written about the happenings, or not?"

The poet-grandson Fahad replied respectfully, "*Labbe*….I have…."

The ninety-year old Sodari tapped him impatiently with a short cane that he had in his hand, and commanded loudly, "You're named after the courageous leopard….so stop squirming like a little girl, and sing!" This comment made all the children in the crowd break out into loud laughter. Among them were his sons and grandsons. It was the beginning of winter and a fire was burning in the centre of the yard in front of the house around which everyone was seated. *Samar* logs were smouldering in the fire and Sodari asked for some *ssaaf* (aromatic grass) to be added to it.

Sodari would order *ssaaf* grass to be added to the fire only on those occasions when his heart was heavy or when guests were present. The *ssaaf* grass grew in the interior of the desert during winter, and he would then instruct his sons to bring bundles of it and store them at home. Because he had wandered as a nomad in the desert in his youth, he knew exactly where the best quality of the grass grew. When added to burning *samar* wood, this *ssaaf* grass would exude such fine fragrance for miles around that our fingers would itch to physically grab hold of it. The scent would be so bewitching that people would wish they had nasal openings all over their bodies. *Qasida*-spouting poets would be so fascinated by its pleasant odour and yield their hearts to it so completely, that the *jinns* would take possession of them totally. One such moment was the trigger point for the war that would commence that day.

Fahad began his recitation:

"How do I sing of the valorous deed of
Zoubi ibn Sodari ibn Naql ibn Deeb Banu Murra al Taqlib,
The son of the fifth wife of the leading light of our al Taqlib kabeela,
Sodari ibn Naql ibn Deeb Banu Murra al Taqlib,
A feat that enhanced the prestige of
That valiant leader of the Banu Murra kabeela of the Al Taqlibs,
Sodari ibn Naql ibn Deeb Banu Murra al Taqlib?
My a'ammi has inherited his valour from my great-great-great-grandfather,
Taqlib,

Who used to stalk the very stars in the desert sky.
Having personally witnessed this exploit I, an unworthy kahin,
As lowly as the grass trampled beneath a camel's feet,
Sing to you of that accomplishment.
"I had expressed a desire to my a'ammi Zoubi of wishing to see
The ancient paths travelled by our ancestors.
Four of us, descendants of my grandfather, Sodari ibn Naql ibn Deeb Banu
Murra al
Taqlib,
Set forth to explore and absorb the sahra into our consciousness
Along with Zoubi ibn Sodari ibn Naql ibn Deeb Banu Murra al Taqlib,
The sixth son of the fifth wife of our kabeela's elder, Sodari ibn Naql ibn Deeb
Banu
Murra al Taqlib,
And also to explore the terrain traversed by our ancestors aeons before us.
We experienced the ramla's (desert's) fierce paternal love that day.
Welcoming us, it bade the wind to cease, allowing us free passage.
If only my words could have captured its beauty during the various phases of time,
My life would have achieved its true meaning. Since that meaning encompasses
the

Lives of all my ancestors, I needed to reclaim it at all costs.

"Having decided this, I made my way, singing my verses.
With my kabeela's kinsmen enthusing me all the way.
We left our maghatirs at the foothills and went up the timeless Jebel Aflaj.
Wasn't that the very spot which had been visited by Hatim ibn Saad al Tai,
The icon of the Tai tribe, which had provided sustenance and saved the life of my
Great-great-great-grandfather?
It was to pay homage at that site that my d'ammi, Zoubi ibn Sodari ibn Naql ibn Deeb Banu Murra Al Taqlib , who is like a second father to me, bade us climb that mountain.
As we climbed, he kept singing of his father's exploits.
And, as Khozama flowers that carpeted the mountainside cushioned our feet all the way,
The life and deeds of our guardian eminence, Sodari ibn Naql ibn Deeb Banu Murra al Taqlib, appeared like a rainbow in front of our eyes -
The desert he had roamed in, the stars that had looked down upon him
And the snakes that he had killed....
We stood at the summit praying to the jebel to grant us a modicum at least of
His large heart that had rushed to offer succour when a famished wolf had let out an
Anguished howl.

"We had an altercation with a group of northern bedus who arrived there,
Asserting our right to be at that spot, by virtue of being bedouins ourselves.
When they failed to vanquish us with their weapons, the cowards challenged us
To a poetry battle, demanding that we recite the history of the mountain.
Being unaware of its lore, and unwilling to make up lies and bring infamy upon my
Ancestors, I declined, hurting internally that the five of us were the cause of
Bringing disrepute to our Banu Murra kabeela.
Accepting that challenge, the son of Sodari ibn Naql ibn Deeb Banu Murra al Taqlib,
Zoubi ibn Sodari ibn Naql ibn Deeb Banu Murra al Taqlib sang about the days when
Jebel Aflaj was first formed, and smiled victoriously at their mortification in defeat.

When he sang the praises of mount Aflaj's beauty over the generations,
Little did we realise that a poetry jinn had taken up residence within him.

"They then invited us to their encampment saying, 'Welcome, welcome,
We are both related by blood. Our ancestry appears to be common.'
It was a very large settlement.
The elders there welcomed us saying, "Harhab, harhab…."
We responded with, "Al Bega, Al Bega…." and, kissing them on their foreheads,
Took our seats.
They asked about our lineage.
And, my a'ammi, Zoubi ibn Sodari ibn Naql ibn Deeb Banu Murra al Taqlib
Began to describe in detail the greatness of our Banu Murra al Taqlib kabeela,
Beginning with its origin and delineating all its ninety generations.
Establishing that he indeed had a poetry jinn inside of him.
It turned out the elders belonged to the Shammari group of bedouins.
One of them said, "We and your Banu Murra kabeela have a long history of
Matrimonial alliances… Arhab, arhab…" and recited a poem of welcome.
They then treated us to a sumptuous feast.
We were also showered with countless gifts along with three maghatir camels
And bidden farewell with warm wishes to our elders by means of another verse.
As we were taking our leave, after politely hailing them as , "Akram min Hatim,"
A few persons belonging to our Banu kabeela who also lived there, having heard
Of our presence, came to invite us to a feast at their camp.
Ignoring our polite demurrals, they insisted we accompany them, and cordially
urging, "Talba, talba…." took us along. It was only after we reached their
encampment, and While exchanging notes about our ancestries we realised that
they belonged to the Descendants of the Isbahs who had fought our ancestor,
Sodari ibn Naql ibn Deeb
Banu Murra al Taqlib, and exiled him.
Before they could reach for their swords, we were flying on our camels.
In the gloom of the waning moon, we plunged them into confusion and went
swimming Far away into the desert.
Apparently our ancestors used to visit al-Hind during monsoons to learn
swimming.
While singing about it, our preceptor, Zoubi ibn Sodari ibn Naql ibn Deeb
Banu Murra

Al Taqlib
Once again plunged us into a state of shock and excitement.
While we were applauding the proud claim by one of us about the spoils he had
Looted from a Isbah household, our a'ammi stunned us into silence.
Two severed male heads dripping with blood were in his right hand!
And a long-haired female in his left!
Not bloodstained,
But shedding tears.
From the Isbah kabeela, which had disrespected our grandfather, he had captured a Female hostage!
We yelled out in acclamation and ululated with joy.
We dissuaded the girl from any thought of running away.
By snipping off her tongue.
Her charms enticed my a'ammi, Zoubi ibn Sodari ibn Naql ibn Deeb Banu Murra al Taqlib
Who hugged and kissed her repeatedly.
In the fading sunlight, we enjoyed the sight of his shenab tickling her face.
She cried,
And whimpered,
Tried to articulate something.

"After initially discarding her in the midst of the desert
We returned to that spot on my a'ammi Zoubi ibn Sodari ibn Naql ibn Deeb Banu Murra al Taqlib's say-so,
Revived her from her faint and gave her a drink of water.
In order to preserve the honour of our kabeela,
The son of the fifth wife of the rock of our kabeela, Sodari ibn Naql ibn Deeb Banu Murra
Al Taqlib, Zoubi ibn Sodari ibn Naql ibn Deeb Banu Murra al Taqlib brought the half-dead
Woman here."

As Fahad ended his recitation, the men in the crowd had let out loud shouts of approbation, the women had ululated in jubilation and Sodari ibn Naql al Taqlib had smiled appreciatively. He then decreed that the poem be taught to all the youngsters in the *kabeela* so that it may be sung for generations to come.

The lady referred to in this epic poem was Zoubi's fifth wife. She was the one who fainted a few minutes before the war commenced. The reason for this had caused Zoubi to shed bitter tears and loathe her from the bottom of his heart.

Before the war broke out, she had been happily watching the dancers, since it was her first experience of attending such an event. As she surreptitiously felt her belly, wondering when she would become pregnant, and mentally revelling in her changed circumstances, the slaves' festivities got off the ground. While the initial burst of music from their dancing shattered the night's silence and caused her insides to thrill, the feeling subsided quickly enough. Even though she could not articulate the fact that Zoubi had snatched her under the mistaken idea that she was the daughter of an enemy, she had tried her best to correct that impression. But Zoubi had been unable to comprehend the garbled sounds that had come out of her mouth. The war revealed her true identity and exposed both her and Zoubi to utter ridicule. Before she collapsed in a dead faint, she had come out with a light heart to watch the slaves' dance performance.

The slaves' dancing was slowly gathering momentum with the accompaniment of their *tablah* and *tar* drums. Their song was proceeding from its refrain, known as *muwwal,* to its main chorus.

Only a few bedouins had any real interest in watching the slaves' uninhibited performance. Most would walk away, not wishing to see them cavorting wildly. The majority of the bedu women would also go back into the houses. Some of the audience would greet the spectacle with jeers and laughter. Only a handful stayed back to actually enjoy the dancing. Bedus only dance to music following a victory in a war. The slaves would usually play their *tablah* and *tar* drums as accompaniments to the war dance, called the *ardha,* and inflame the bedus into a wild frenzy. They would then dance a frenetic jig together and celebrate their victory. Since their music was indispensable at such times, the slaves were allowed to dance with their masters on those occasions.

A few of Sodari's sons, along with his first-born, were seated in the yard watching the festivities. Sodari's favourite son, and the slaves' champion, Zoubi, was standing a little apart in the gloom with a group of bedouin poets. It was his usual practice to watch the slaves' *saamri* dancing from a distance. He was also in the habit of resolving any disputes that arose between the slaves and the bedouins on such occasions.

Once the *tablah* drum heads had been tuned by warming them over the open campfire, they began to sound their basic "tak....taka.... tak....tak" rhythm. The drummers began to display their virtuosity by dancing in time to the rhythm and swinging the *tablahs* up and down over their shoulders as their fingers worked their magic. Another group of slaves began to sing a poem in time with the tempo of the drums. Some ten to fifteen *tablahs* began competing with the poetry's lines and made the night throb with their cadence. The sound, that synchronised with the listeners' heartbeats, spread like a rainbow throughout the night and permeated their souls. The booming sound of the *tars* thundered in everyone's ears in an attempt to overshadow the bedouins' earlier songs as though underlining the plain nature of their performance. Some of the Black musicians seemed to be frenziedly pounding their drums as though mentally challenging, 'match this with your own bland, lacklustre performance!'

As if they had been waiting for the right opportunity, the dancing *jinns* entered the bodies of the slaves and took control. Waving their hands about and jerking their legs, they were impelled into a frenzy of spontaneous unrestricted movement. Like some of the bedouin poets, the dancing slaves too appeared to have offered up opiates to the *jinns* and ceded total control of their bodies to them.

Those slaves who did not participate in the performance continued to tend to their masters' needs and ensured they enjoyed this mad jig by their companions.

Mesmerised by the magic of their music, a few bedouins would join the Blacks in their dancing and leap about maniacally. But most, well aware that they could not match the Blacks in their efforts, preferred to stand to one side and savour the slaves' gyrations.

Two groups of men would kneel facing each other and sing their compositions, swaying their bodies side to side rhythmically, while a group of drummers would sit in a circle around the campfire and provide the accompaniment. The initial pack of four or five dancers, who acted as a bridge between the two groups, would grow in size as the drumming increased in tempo. The singing and the pounding of the drums would add fuel to the dancing *jinns'* efforts to attain the peak of their endeavour. The remaining dancing *jinns* watching the performance of their compatriots within the bodies of humans, and unable to withstand their impulse, would hasten to enter the bodies of those favoured by them. At such times, they would not differentiate between slaves and bedouins, but generally preferred the Blacks.

Some of the slaves were dancing uninhibitedly, without caring about the difference in their ages. Their bodies twisted uncontrollably in the wind in time to the wild drum beats. The Black poets then began a song about the physical aspect of love, a composition that had come down to them over generations. It had been Sodari's favourite number. When the slaves sang that piece, he would walk up to the performer, kiss him on his brow and present him with whatever was in his possession. It was that poem that the slaves belonging to the Banu Murra *kabeela* of the Taqlib bedouins now struck up.

At the end of the poem, the drumming of the *tablah* would reach a crescendo and pause for a while. It was at that moment when the *jinns* that had been lurking in the darkness all this while would enter their chosen humans and cause them to lose all control of themselves.

As usual, when the climax of the poem and the peak of the drumming were reached that day, the bodies of the performing slaves appeared to balloon and swell and threaten the very darkness around them. The slaves held in thrall by the *jinns* appeared to have totally abandoned their bodies to the influence of the spirits. The dancing *jinns* were in complete possession of the men's bodies and were swinging and twisting them to their will.

As the bedouins watched in awe, wondering if they were special *jinns* exclusive to the world of slaves, the spirits resident within the bodies of two black slaves caused them to leap about madly, roll their eyes maniacally, and thrust their tongues out menacingly. While some of the spectators laughed at their antics, a few could not help but stare awestruck at this display. Some of the bedouin children, scared out of their wits, hid behind their fathers' legs and peered out in fear.

More than ten slaves were being activated by *jinns*. A docile slave, who was quietly serving tea to the watching bedouins, was suddenly seized by a *jinn* with a roar, and thrown violently to the ground.

The sudden, unprovoked attack was viewed with utter consternation by both the bedouins and the slaves. That was because the young man involved had never once in all his life ventured to sing or dance. Throughout his life all he had ever done was carry out his masters' orders to the best of his ability. Even his normal speech, like his father's, was in a soft, muted cadence. This had earned him barbs and slights from many of his friends and relatives. No one in his circle had ever heard him raise his voice on any issue. In fact, his soft nature had earned him harsh words from his own mother. There had been occasions when she had lost patience with him and angrily berated him saying his paternal uncle would never give him his daughter in marriage if the youngster's attitude did not change. His father however had repeatedly dinned it into him that he should obey his masters implicitly and be subservient to their wishes. He had also been constantly told that he should strictly avoid drinking and cavorting like a maniac, like some of his compatriots did. He had scrupulously followed that dictum and had on more than one occasion been praised for being 'just like his father' by his masters, which had gladdened his heart no end. At 25 years of age, he had never before participated in the slaves' dances. The *jinns* had also left him alone until now. But, just minutes before the war commenced, one of them had entered him and hurled him to the ground.

Zoubi was standing to one side along with his bedouin poets and enjoying a quiet laugh at this sight. Of the fifteen-odd bedouins standing around there, only a few were watching the young man dancing. The slaves however viewed the young man's performance with considerable surprise. The *tar* drums were being pounded furiously while the slaves' singing reached its peak.

The young man knelt on all his fours and arched his body like a bow. It was not he who was performing the feat - it was the *jinn* inside him activating him. Did he really possess the power within himself to overawe all those watching him perform? The *jinn* seemed keen on extracting every bit of energy stored inside him over all these years.

The young man sprang up in the air, floated there for a while before landing on the ground with both feet planted firmly. Moving his hands sinuously in time to the beat of the *tar* drums, he began slowly gyrating his body. Those who had been watching him awestricken, let out a collective breath and began keenly observing his movements. The bedouins around watched him open-eyed. Another shock then awaited them. The father of the young man suddenly joined him in the dancing. The portly man's movements provoked much laughter among the *bedus*. His dancing to the frantic beats of the *tablah* drums, shaking his barrel-like belly and hips, reminded them of an elephant from *al-Hind* cavorting in the desert, and caused much hilarity among the spectators.

In the meantime, the young man confronted his paternal uncle, who was playing the *tar*, and, as though challenging him to a contest, began to swing his head violently and dance in a never-before-seen manner. His uncle, not to be outdone, began playing the *tar* in sync with his novel movements. The song in progress now reflected the pain of a forsaken lover.

Finally, the uncle had to concede defeat to the youngster and abandon his drumming. The other *tar* and *tablah* players, however, impelled by the *jinns,* were progressing towards the peak of their drumming.

The young man was twirling like the wind. Some slaves stood by, apprehensive that the *jinn* was unlikely to let go of him, and were biding their time to cover his face with a piece of cloth and drag him away when the music reached its crescendo.

The throats giving voice to the songs grew from ten to twenty to a hundred as they started a new *muwwal* paying homage to the *jinns*. The *tars* and the *tablahs* would remain silent till the refrain ended, but the underlying beat of the *tablah* would resonate with the dancers' heartbeats and enable them to merge with the *jinns*. The young man, however, was showing signs of becoming heated at the time of the *muwwal* itself. Some considered that the *jinn* which possessed him would exit his body after raising him to feverish heights after the completion of that song. As the *muwwal* continued, several spectators kept shouting, "Oy, oy oy…." in order to further inflame the *jinn* within him. The *jinn* activated the youth's head up and down and was waiting for the rest of the *tar* drums to start sounding. As soon as their drumming commenced, the *jinn* began to leap about wildly and subjected the young man's body to indescribable torment. His father, unable to bear his son's torment, shouted out, "You're inflicting untold agony on my son, you *jinn*! Leave him alone…." The *jinn* glared at him with bloodshot eyes, thrust its tongue out threateningly and gnashed its teeth in anger. Thrusting out its chest and shaking it from side to side, and swinging its head wildly, it leaped about with abandon. The *tar* drums reached another peak as they attempted to charm the *jinns.*

The *jinn* that was inside the young man now began to take in deep breaths as though the inhalation via the human lungs would reach and enter the very core of its soul and, while noisily exhaling and pumping its chest, glanced at the singers as though saying 'this music isn't good enough'. Everyone around was aware that the *jinn* wouldn't depart from the man's body until the music attained its peak. Some of the spectators eagerly awaited to see what further torment the *jinn* was going to inflict upon the young man.

Anticipating the *jinn*'s moves, the Black singers began a refrain of 'lalalala' and commenced a *muwwal* to match its ferocious jig. The *tar* and *tablah* drums had been given a breather. It was common for the *jinns* to refuse to vacate the human bodies they had taken possession of until the final battle jig was performed. They would express this intention not by words but through certain bodily movements. The black poets who realise this belatedly, would ask the poetry *jinns* within them to emerge, unbeknownst to their masters, and give them opium and create a new world with their aid.

They would also sing the battle hymn of the *jinn* world in one voice. The dancing *jinns* would be so enchanted by the magical words of the singing *jinns,* totally incomprehensible to human ears, that both would engage in a battle between song and dance. When the singing reached its climax, some of the *jinns* would leave the bodies of the slaves and, satisfied with the engagement, depart for their motherland of Abqer Wadi.

Such a battle hymn was commencing there on that day. As soon as the first line of the poem sounded, several bedus rose from their seats. They were not keen on staying back to witness the mad caper that the black slaves would engage in. It was usual for them to walk away when the finale of the jig was reached. It was the Blacks who would give a respectful send-off to the *jinns* who had come to the human world.

The *jinns* occupying men's bodies were in the habit of using their fingers, which they would extend like swords, to kill their enemies who roamed in the wind, and pile their bodies in a heap. They would trample over the bodies of their enemies, who were visible to their eyes alone, and set them alight. The bedouins would leave at this stage not wishing to witness this scene when the slaves' wild frenzy peaked. In keeping with this practice, the bedus got up that day too, not wishing to watch the climax of their slaves' dance.

It was then that the *jinn* possessing the young slave roared in anger and stood blocking the bedouins' path with its eyes rolling in fury and plunging them into panic. As they were terrified at this sudden transformation caused by a fearful *jinn* within a peaceable and gentle person, a further shock awaited them. The *jinn* thrust its tongue out menacingly, gnashed its teeth, swivelled its head alarmingly and spun its eyes in a terrifying manner causing the eyeballs to roll into its head displaying only the whites of the eyes to the petrified spectators. It seemed to be saying to the panic-stricken bedouins, 'watch the rest of our performance also, you earthlings'. Among them were Sodari's first and second sons. The terror-struck first son quickly held on to his brothers and tried to hide behind them. Some of the slaves, believing that the *jinn* had attained its peak, rushed forward to cover the young man's face with a piece of cloth and drag him away. At this, the *jinn* inside the youth roared in anger causing the slaves to pause in their tracks. It then extended its fingers like swords and charged towards the bedouins. At that very instant, Zoubi ibn Sodari, wielding his real live sword, came hurtling through the darkness, slashed the youngster's head off and kicked his lifeless body aside. Blood spurted from the young man's severed throat with a hissing sound.

As Zoubi ibn Sodari uttered his next words, the entire assembly froze in silence. Some lowered their eyes, scared to even meet his eyes as he yelled out. He raised the bloodstained sword aloft and shouted:

"No one is greater here than us bedouins. Whether God, *jinn* or black dogs - everyone is but our slave." He then turned to his elder brother and instructed his other brothers, "Ya rajel, escort him safely inside...." Even the dark of the night seemed to tremble at the sound of his voice.

Even as some slaves wondered if a *jinn* had entered Zoubi ibn Sodari's body as well, others prayed for the night to end soon. They had never in their wildest imagination believed that the favourite son of the elder Sodari, Zoubi ibn Sodari, would end up killing one of their youngsters. They had believed all along that, like the senior Sodari, Zoubi would also always be on their side.

As night fell and enveloped them totally, the slaves heard the *jinns* within some of them leave their host bodies with loud shouts and cackling.

"Bury him after the feast," instructed Zoubi ibn Sodari al Taqlib to the slaves sternly. Then, turning to his group of young bedouin poets, he added jovially, "Hey guys! Come along; let's eat." They stood there stunned at his transformation. The man who had been joking and laughing with them all this while had suddenly turned into a brutal killer. While they could not wrap their heads around this sudden role reversal, one thing was very clear. No one could read a bedouin's mind - it could melt one moment while freezing the next. But what they could not fathom also was the very same dual mindset among the Blacks.

They sat down in a circle for feasting.

A whole sheep stuffed with a wheat preparation was served on a large platter. The animal's head was laid towards the East in honour of the visiting guests. The leader of the *kabeela*, Sodari's eldest son, was seated at the North side of the first salver along with ten other elders. The trigger point for the war was reached within ten seconds after all the guests gathered around the trays commenced eating.

As the black slaves attended to the needs of their masters and were looking forward to eating the scraps of the meal left over after the bedouins finished, the flash point for the war was reached.

A raiding party belonging to the Isbah *kabeela* had attacked a settlement in Tamra where the sons of Sodari's third and sixth wives lived, ransacked it and set it on fire. A few months back, the son of Sodari's fifth wife, Zoubi ibn Sodari, had killed two Isbahs and carried off a girl belonging to their *kabeela*. It was widely believed by all those present that this cowardly act was in retaliation to that incident.

But that had been over a year ago. It was only while they were clamouring for revenge on the grounds that, instead of reacting immediately to Zoubi's action, it was cowardly on the part of the Isbahs to stage the raid now, disrespecting our elder's passing, that the shocking revelation came to light. The girl Zoubi had kidnapped, thinking she was an Isbah, was in reality a camp follower, a prostitute. That was the reason why the Isbahs had not taken immediate retaliatory action. The reason for the present raid was something else altogether, it appeared.

As soon as they heard this, some of the womenfolk began to snigger at the girl Zoubi had kidnapped. A few reacted with anger and disgust. At that critical moment, Zoubi's fourth wife delivered a baby boy and fell into a swoon. A slave woman quickly picked up the newborn baby and rushed to the group of bedouin women desperately requesting one of them to suckle the infant. For some reason, none of them were lactating. With no other recourse left to her, the buxom slave hugged the baby to her generous bosom, weeping and bemoaning the fact that she was forced to suckle a bedouin baby. The bedouin women were so busy mocking, reviling and laughing at Zoubi's fifth wife that they paid no heed to his fourth wife who had just delivered. Unable to respond to the insults and being able to counter only with unintelligible babble, Zoubi's favourite fifth wife could only beat her chest and weep bitterly before fainting dead away.

In the yard, the men squabbled, shouted and finally reached a consensus to go to war. The fighting force, the *gazu*, came flying in. Even though Zoubi immersed himself into the preparations for war and was racing on his camel, he could still hear the laughter from his brothers ringing in his ears. Even as he tried hard to despise the girl, memories of her soft breasts, supple thighs and the fragrant heart of her femininity brought tears to his eyes.

Soon, however, his tears dried up amidst the war cries.

12

Rajendran woke up with a start. It took him a few moments to orient himself and get his bearings.

He got off the bed, switched on the fan, removed his shirt and threw it aside. He then checked the time. It was midnight. The rattle of the air-conditioners running in the main hall only seemed to aggravate the humidity inside his room. As they were ancient Decker air-conditioners, the sound of their clatter was ear-splitting. Just as air-conditioners were indispensable during summer months, you couldn't go to sleep without heaters during winter. Both seasons were extreme in this part of the world.

As he had been locked up inside the room, the cool air from the air-conditioners in the hall did not reach him. He tried banging on the door. Everyone was sleeping soundly. As there was no way they could hear his shouts over the sound of the air-conditioners, he turned the fan on full speed and opened the windows to his room.

The sound of someone conversing outside bloomed in the bed of the night's darkness, and its scent captivated his attention. He placed his ear against the wall and eavesdropped shamelessly.

His boss, and cousin, Sundar was speaking to his wife on his phone using the Emo video app. Their conversation sounded to him like honey being poured into his ears. Mentally laughing at Sundar's stupidity in not using earphones while holding an intimate tete-a-tete with his wife, Rajendran settled down to enjoy their lascivious heart-to-heart chat.

Sundar was making vicarious love to his wife over the mobile phone. Out of a total of seven years' married life, he had spent exactly one and a half years with her. Even during that short period, he had spent several days away from her, and ended up wasting those nights as well. Since coming here, he has also rued those nights he had spent alone following some silly spat or the other between them. The thoughts of his three months' holiday back home, when he did not spare her body even during the ten days she needed to be sequestered, tormented him now.

He would burn with longing at nights. He would yearn for the unique experience that was the intermingling of two bodies. His body would thirst for lightning to strike his heart. He would bemoan the compulsion of having to earn money that forced him to live on his own in a foreign land. He had even cursed himself for living and working in a country that did not condone prostitution. At such times, it was his mobile phone that came to his aid. The screens of the mobiles would fulfil both their longings. It would unite them together and cause their bodies to explode. At a stroke of their fingertips, the golden touch that was buried deep within their memories would cast a spell over their eyes and tug the tranquillity that was lying dormant inside them out into the open. This is how their bodies, transcending the distance and the oceans separating them, were now entwined via the web. These conversations normally took place in the toilet. But today it was happening on the porch outside the building. Lying on the verandah just below the window of the room where Rajendran was confined, Sundar was weaving his magical spell. He was so completely immersed in the conversation that he had forgotten all about Rajendran's presence. His side of the conversation which pierced the night's darkness, vibrated against Rajendran's eardrums and titillated him.

"Hold the phone properly.....hmm....hmm....turn around.....bend down.....I've been parched for the last four years....chasing after money, I've lost all of life's pleasures....I know, your position is also the same....spread your legs a bit more....stop! Hold it like that.... bring the phone down a little....a bit more.....ha....that's it....hold it right there....hmm....hmm....hold it a while longer.....hmm.... hmm....hahaha....

"I'm told such things are freely available in America.... ....and they would be identical to yours....no, they are not meant for women.... only for us, males....hmm....hmm....hold it, don't move....hmmm.... turn around and hold the camera up....hmm....whoa....oooffff..... hmm... okay, put your dress back on....I'll go and wash my hand..... hmm....everyone's asleep....wait....I'll be back...."

Having witnessed his cousin's on-line mating, Rajendran quietly shut the window and switched off the light in his room. After wiping his hands on a tissue, he went back to the window and stood by the wall with his ears cocked. They continued their conversation.

"I'm certain he's the thief....when the Arab came to the garage there was no one else around.... he was the only one there....hmm, hmm.... the Arab himself said that the bag had been in the car....this fellow is a crook....mmm....yes, I know....he's just like his father....the old man is also exactly like him....lies, lies, lies, every time he opens his mouth, only lies come out....we've given him time till tomorrow....let's see what he does....if he doesn't confess, we've planned to hand him over to the police....no, don't worry....I'll take care over here....you take care of your end....knowing his mother, she'll come and create a ruckus at our house....you are to deny knowledge of anything, if you're asked....hmm....hmm....don't be scared....nothing will happen....just wait and watch….if he doesn't confess and return the cash tomorrow on his own….hmm….that's right….okay….don't go anywhere near that fellow's house at all….hmm…yes, I know….and, one more thing, don't go near Radha *akka*'s (elder sister) house either….because I say so….stop asking why and wherefore....just stay quietly in the house and don't go gallivanting into the fields for cutting grass and all that stuff….mom will take care of all that….galli….galli….what's wrong with my saying gallivanting….you silly cunt….listen to me….hey… hey….okay, forget it….I said forget it….have the children eaten? Hmmmm…..when I came there the younger one was just three weeks old….what kind of life is this…..it seems vacations are meant only to produce children….hmmm ….don't worry, I'll come back for good soon….just hang on for two more years….that's what I said….two more years….no, I'm not upset with you….no, I tell you, I"m not…. stop repeating yourself….all right, go back to bed…..you need to get up early tomorrow morning….all right, all right….. after I return, the four of us will start a life together separately….we'll construct a small house in the plot given to us by your parents…..okay, we'll begin construction next year itself….I can't afford it right now….I don't have a penny to my name….why don't you understand? Am I a doctor or an engineer, earning millions in a foreign country? I am a mere mechanic….okay go to bed now….we'll talk again tomorrow….. what? Window? What window? Behind me? Wait, let me check…."

Sundar rose, and peered through the window of the room where Rajendran was confined. Rajendran lay face down on his bed. He closed the window softly and resumed his conversation with his wife. Inside, Rajendran stuffed a fist into his mouth and stifled his laughter.

"Hmm…it's him inside….he's sleeping….that room has no AC…. that's why he's sleeping with the window open….no, no….he can't hear us inside the room….hmm…yes….him? We've kept him locked up inside that room….he can't escape….we did it just to intimidate him….this is not India where he can just up and leave….his *iqama* is with me....so, even if he escapes, the police will nab him....the law of this land is very strict.....wait till tomorrow,,,,he'll get his comeuppance....if he doesn't return the money he has stolen, he's done for....when the police slap him around a bit, he'll come clean on his own....if it's proven he is the thief, they will cut off his hand.... where will he go then? Didn't his father, that rogue, swear up and down that his son was a pure soul and I'm levelling these allegations only to malign their family? And he calls himself my uncle? He's the one who hit my father with a shovel....and don't talk to me about his grandma, that hag.... She's the one who instigates all the trouble between our families....she deserves to be killed....bitch! Wait till I come there on my next vacation....see if I don't poison her to death.... hahaha.....no, I'm not joking....all right go to bed now....and don't forget, if this fellow's father, that rogue, or his mother, that bitch, call you names, you've my full authority to retaliate with a broomstick....!"

An infuriated Rajendran rose from the bed.

"Who're you calling a bitch, you bastard? Your mother is a raddled whore....you fucking asshole, you dare call my mother a bitch? Wait and watch....if I don't fist your wife's hole, I'm not my father's son ...."

As he went towards the door to bang on it, his telephone rang. He picked it up. It was a call from Ahmed *bhai*. Rajendran was supposed to have stolen money from him as well.

Why is that fucker calling at this time of the night?

An aggravated Rajendran yelled in frustration as he hurled the telephone away in disgust.

13

A smattering of stars were visible in the night sky. Seated on his camel, Sodari looked up at the tenth day moon.

He breathed in the deep scent of the vast Najd desert. All around were towering sand dunes that seemed to reach up to the skies. Sodari ibn Naql ibn Deeb Banu Murra al Taqlib ar Rabiya loved to stand on top of tall drifts inhaling the fragrance of the stars. That day too he was seated on his favourite light brown camel atop a towering sand dune. The camel train of his tribesmen was seen snaking its way in the distance. It was a vast desolate stretch of the desert where not a drop of water was available. Known as the "Empty Quarter" or the *Rub' al Khali*, the terrain was covered with soaring sand dunes as far as the eye could see. A constant drift of sand in the ever-present winds. A searingly hot plain with no water in sight. The region sizzles during summers while its winters are bitterly cold.

The caravan was making its way through the sky-high dunes to the nearest oasis. Some of the travellers were singing *mankoos* songs to relieve the tedium of travel. They would camp for a few days at the nearest spot offering water and fodder for their camels before proceeding further on their way.

Some of the rootless *bedus,* constantly on the move, wished to settle down permanently at a suitable spot and engage in agriculture. But this idea did not appeal to the group belonging to Sodari ibn Naql ibn Deeb Banu Murra al Taqlib. They feared that such a move might endanger the growth and future development of their offspring and their camel herds.

They were well aware of when the heat would be at its fiercest, when the desert would experience the freezing *sheeta* (winter wind) and when the *obaar* (sandstorm) would start blowing. They knew from experience which parts of the desert would provide protection during the different seasons. Instead of staying at one spot permanently, they constantly roved the vast expanse of the desert heading towards water sources.

The area was about a thousand miles long. At most, the group would stay at one spot for two months at a time and then, depending upon the position of the stars, proceed towards their next destination. In keeping with this practice, Sodari ibn Naql ibn Deeb Banu Murra al Taqlib was now leading his caravan towards another oasis.

It was winter and the start of the season called *vassaam*. Winter in the desert is harsh. Nights were no ordinary times. A bone-numbingly chill wind would blow through the land. It was enough to vanquish the heat of summer. It was during the beginning of such a winter month that the caravan was proceeding from the South to the North of the desert. If they feared the cold and took shelter, they worried that their children might grow up to be cowardly weaklings, and so were boldly undertaking the trip. Their aim was to reach the *wadi* (valley) before the cold season ended. Their intention was to commence their journey when winter started and complete it by arriving at the *wadi* before the season ended, so that they may joyfully welcome the first rain at the destination. By the time the second rains came, grass would grow in abundance over there. It would make good fodder for their camels. The camels would produce sweet, creamy milk after grazing on the new, lush grass. Drinking that milk would give humans an extraordinary boost of energy. It would provide their lovemaking an extra impetus, and titillate even the most prosaic of minds. It was a firm belief among certain bedus that, among all other creatures, only the camel possessed the capability to restore lost feelings within a human's body.

Perched atop the sand dune, Sodari ibn Naql ibn Deeb Banu Murra al Taqlib was studying the sky.

The big star that usually makes its appearance in the western sky during the second part of the night had not yet shown itself. Only when it appears will his route become clearer.

He studied the sky carefully. The moon appeared to be within his grasp. It was clear that a sand storm was in the offing within the next two to three days.

A small star named *tamar* was making its way eastwards across the sky. It was the one star that provided them with every information they needed. It was the indicator that signalled rain, wind and heat to the bedus. Their calculations of how long to camp in a particular site were based on the signs indicated by that star.

Bedus called that life-saving star *tamar* or 'date'. Just as the fruit that bore its name nourished them in the desert, they considered this star their guiding light in the sky. The star would be clearly visible on full moon days. After indicating the course of the next fifteen days, it would gradually fade away. The bedus would not make a move on moonless nights.

The *tamr* was clearly visible in the vast emptiness of the *Rub' al Khali*. Everywhere you looked were towering sand dunes variously called *yerg, taiyis* or *ghose*. It was a space where no vegetation grew and not a single drop of water was available. However, herds of desert deer named Al Maha occasionally roamed in the wilderness.

Sodari ibn Naql al Taqlib has seen groups of the deer darting across sand dunes on full moon nights. He had also occasionally hunted them for their meat. But that was an infrequent occurrence. He would however invariably pick up and store their droppings. He continued the bedouin tradition of making aromatic pellets called *misk* from these pellets.

He would grow enraged at the sight of foxes howling from atop sand dunes and would immediately target them with his arrows.

If they passed by silently, he would simply watch them from his perch on top of his camel. He would however not spare any wolf that caught his eye.

The minute he spotted a wolf pack, he would unleash a barrage of arrows at them. If he caught sight of a wolf that was intent on stealing one of his lambs, he would immediately burn with anger. He would take it as a personal challenge and would not rest until he had killed the predator.

While he was once camped at a *wadi*, a wolf strayed into the settlement to grab one of his lambs. As one of its legs was injured, it had come limping into the pen. While there, it had stumbled, fallen and broken another of its legs also. It lay on the ground twitching in agony.

Sodari ibn Naql al Taqlib, who noticed this incident, picked up the animal, tended to its injuries, fed it for two days and then, when it regained some of its strength, released it back in the mountains.

In contrast to this episode, a pack of wolves had once descended upon his settlement. That was when some kinsmen from afar had dropped in for a visit.

The guests were enjoying a feast consisting of a large camel specially slaughtered for the occasion when a pack of some ten to fifteen wolves were sighted coming down the mountains. One of the guests who spotted them, shouted out a warning to safeguard the sheep and rushed out to hunt the raiders.

Sodari ibn Naql al Taqlib had restrained him saying, "You're our honoured guest. It's our duty to ensure your comfort and wellbeing," and, accompanied by his own kinsmen and sons, had hurried to hunt the animals down. During that skirmish, one of the wolves had charged at him and pushed him down to the ground. Since that day, wolves had been his sworn enemies.

He therefore watched keenly for any signs of wolves. But there were no deer, foxes or wolves to be seen anywhere in the vicinity.

He sharpened his ears and let them float in the wind. He could hear no sound of human activity. He smelt the air for any scent of bedouin bandits, but none was discernible. Since he himself had engaged in dacoity, he did not fear these brigands. Presented with an opportunity he was not the one to shy away from highway robbery. While he believed that such raids and looting were treasures offered to them by *jinns*, it was not his habit to engage in such activities every time. In fact, he had personally provided protection to several trade caravans crossing the desert.

He went up yet another tall sand dune and looked up at the moon which presented an appearance of a dented silver plate. His heart contracted a bit.

He looked down. None of his kinsmen were visible. "*Sura Ya rajjal.* Hurry up...." he called out to them.

This was normal practice while negotiating sand dunes. Plus this was a different route. They could not be left behind either lest they lost their way. Bedouins never followed one fixed route while traversing the desert. They followed different paths while travelling back and forth.

To reach a destination a second time, they would not take the same route as the previous occasion. They would explore a new trail. It was the stars that charted their course to their destination, not the land route. They held the view that anyone who consistently followed just one course possessed the intellect of a donkey!

The camel, which would return to them on its own from any corner of the desert, was their ideal.

They were also in awe of its capacity to store water within its body and absorb it whenever needed. It was their firm belief that no other creature on earth possessed such a capability. Having grown up listening to fables about camels, the animal was dearer to them than life itself.

Sodari ibn Naql ibn Deeb Banu Murra al Taqlib had heard one such story during his childhood. That tale was still fresh in his mind.

Once a camel crossed the desert and ventured into a forest. On the way, it encountered an injured animal. It helped the wounded beast to somehow reach its lair. It was only after they arrived at the destination did the camel realise that the animal it had helped was none other than a lion, the king of beasts. The camel grew somewhat apprehensive.

But the king lion thanked the camel and asked it to stay back. Disregarding all protests by the camel that the forest was not its natural habitat, the lion persuaded the camel to remain and continue to be its best friend. The camel too began considering the lion its boon companion.

A sudden drought affected the region. Most animals migrated to other fertile locations. Only the lion king's mate and a small retinue consisting of a fox and a wolf were left behind, along with the camel.

Food and water became scarce. The camel however continued to thrive. Seeing this, the wolf and the fox went up to the lion king and suggested, "Oh king....if you kill this camel, we'll all be saved from hunger. There would be enough meat to last us all for at least a week. Please consider our suggestion. We can sustain ourselves until the rains come and the other regular prey animals return to the forest."

The lion king who was initially incensed at this suggestion was slowly brought around by his lioness. She also suggested to the wolf and the fox the best way to kill the camel without overtly upsetting the king.

As per her plan, the camel was brought before her. The lioness, shedding fake tears, implored the animals, "Friends, our king is suffering desperately from hunger pangs.... we need to save him at any cost, even if it means giving up our own lives.....please let me have your suggestions...."

The fox immediately spoke up, "My queen, only the king is capable of protecting our forest.... he therefore needs to be kept alive no matter what....here, I'm ready to be his meal, if that's what it takes....please go ahead and kill me."

The wolf laughed at this and commented, "You'll make a tasty snack, I grant you that. But that's about it....oh, queen, take me instead.... my flesh will feed the king for at least two days...."

Listening to the others, the camel lifted his neck slightly and, thrusting out its lips, trying to control its own tears, said in a trembling voice, "Oh, queen! Please offer my body to the king.... I'm aware he loves me more than life itself, but he needs to stay alive....I'm ready to give up my life in order to save him....all of you can feast on my body for several days....please call the king .... ask him to crush my neck and kill me...." So saying, the camel extended its neck forward.

Unable to meet his friend's eyes, a weeping lion king rushed out of its lair. As the other animals watched, he charged at the camel, clamped his jaws around its throat and broke its neck. The camel gazed fondly at the lion one last time before slumping down on the ground dead.

This story had been told to Sodari ibn Naql ibn Deeb Banu Murra al Taqlib by his grandfather.

Since that day, he had become very attached to camels. He had decided mentally that he would live like the camel and even give up his life, if necessary, for those who trusted him. When he was a ten-year old child, some distant relatives had come calling at their settlement. There was nothing to feed them with at home then. It was a time of terrible drought in the land. All their livestock, including camels and goats, had died of hunger by then. The land was reeling with terrible thirst with not a drop of water being available.

As the family worried about how to entertain the visitors in the absence of any food, the ten-year old Sodari ibn Naql had walked up to his father and said, "Father, I'm your eldest son....stronger than all my brothers....kill me and serve me up to the guests so that my father may not suffer the ignominy of being unable to extend proper hospitality to our guests....please cut off my head," and had stretched out his neck.

To their surprise, however, the visitors declared, "We're only here to deliver a supply of corn and meat to you in response to our grandfather's - your grandfather's brother's - instructions. He has somehow sensed that your area is suffering from a severe drought and that your family is facing starvation. He therefore asked us to bring these supplies to you." They then handed over two sacks of corn and a whole slaughtered lamb wrapped in cloth to Sodari's father, Naql ibn Deeb Banu Murra al Taqlib.

So far in his life he has encountered three periods of drought. He has boldly faced up to the catastrophes in his childhood and in his fortieth year. With not a drop of rain and the landscape burning up like an oven, he had courageously met the desert head-on while some of his kinsfolk and camels dropped dead around him. The will to survive burned fiercely like a torch within him. He had looked in vain to spot a trade caravan within his territory. He had fretted that there had been no opportunities to either rob one or to offer them his protection services. While highway robbery was some bedouins' way of life, Sodari had employed it only once or twice in his lifetime.

More often than not, he provided protection to merchants plying on the trade routes. He had lost both these opportunities during times of drought, and had agonised over his inability to safeguard his kinfolk at such times. He had also on such occasions felt furious enough to want to do battle with the relentless sun if he could only lay his hands on it. To alleviate that feeling he would immediately rush southwards with his kinsmen to where the tillers of land, known as the *hadaris,* lived, and proceed to sack their settlements. The age-old conflict between nomads and settlers would assume monstrous proportions during periods of drought. Whatever protective measures the agriculturists put in place for their safety, the nomads would breach them with contemptuous ease, loot the settlements and escape into the bosom of the desert with lightning speed. The settlers would be left with no option but to bemoan their losses ineffectually. Having learnt these tactics from his grandfather, Sodari employed them to great effect during times of hardship, and managed to somehow take care of his tribesmen.

Having crossed the final sand dune, Sodari ibn Naql al Taqlib was proceeding towards an oasis along with his kinsfolk.

"We have done enough roving. Let's settle here permanently with our camels and provide our children with a stable life," he declared.

One of his cousins demurred, "We'd make it easy for brigands if we stayed put at one spot."

"We have bows, arrows and swords. Our people are courageous and can resist any raid boldly. We'll also send some of our young men to *Hind* and bring back the best swords they have on offer. I have seen some of their swords. They last a long time and are extremely sharp. If we had ten such swords it would be sufficient to take on not just marauders but also anyone who dares to meddle with us. They are such great *saifs* (swords). We can offer our finest horses in exchange for them," Sodari said.

Everyone seemed to agree with their commander's statement. Some began to discuss the best route to take to *Hind* and which horses were to be offered in exchange for the arms.

A young man raised a question. "You talk a lot about *Hind*.... Where is it exactly?"

Sodari ibn Naql ibn Deeb Banu Murra al Taqlib smiled at the young man and replied, "It's a land of plenty. Everything is available there.... the perfumed *oud* that we use is from there. It is a wonderful place. A fertile land where the skies offer up regular rains. The people there venerate idols just like our ancestors used to do. That's why we named their land *Hind*. You know what the word '*Hind*' means, don't you? Though it means 'beautiful' in our language, I personally have a different interpretation. I am of the opinion that our people named it *Hind* because the *Hindis* worship idols just like our forefathers did. I suggest you accompany the group that goes there on the sword-buying mission. When you return, I expect you to sing a *qasida* about the places you visited and the people you met during your trip."

He continued, "Along with the magnificent swords, I want you to also bring back a supply of rice, pepper and wheat. Let this young poet accompany our experienced *kahins* who are well aware of the route to *Hind*. Let him compose new poems including those which describe the route to *Hind*. This would help our coming generations to learn of the passage to *Hind*. While there, pass on some of our poems to the poets of *al-Hind* and pick up some of their compositions in turn. Send ten *asmar* slaves with the group. Let them take the land route on the way out and return partly by sea and partly via land. Our poems talk of sea routes that are safe from pirates. If the poets who know them are not among us, look for them among our kinsmen's *kabeelas*. As mentioned in those poems, they can land at Sana'a and make their way to Najd via Aseer. And don't forget to caution the poets....they should carefully bring back their memories of the voyage, recording the adventures of each day, the direction travelled and their everyday experiences without fail. Before you proceed, I'll sing the composition that speaks of the position of the stars as a guide.... Let the young poet then expand on it."

At this, two cousins from his paternal side voiced a suggestion.

"Why don't we bring goods from *Hind* and trade in them ourselves at Sana'a and Mecca? After all, people of our *kabeela* are well aware of the route to *Hind*. Currently, the non-bedouins dominate the trade in these commodities. They merely employ us to provide them with protection during their voyage, and reap huge profits by bringing in the goods to these parts. All we do when we visit *Hind* is to procure essential supplies for ourselves. Why don't we start trading in them ourselves? Since we roam the desert all our lives, crossing lands is no big deal for us."

Upon hearing this, Sodari ibn Naql ibn Deeb Banu Murra al Taqlib became highly incensed.

"Our wants are limited to what we need till next summer. This is the norm we have followed over generations. Our ancestors have modelled their lives on the *ramla* (desert) and the *ibil* (camel). It does not befit a bedouin to lead the life of a sedentary coward. If we did so, we would become the laughingstock of our kinsmen. Beyond everything else, it is our bounden duty to revere everything that our ancestors held sacred. I'll not permit anyone to breach these unwritten rules. I too consider myself bound by these bedouin laws. If any of you plan to do anything to the contrary, it will result in a bloodbath." After making this angry pronouncement, he began to follow a camel that was about to give birth, fearing it might deliver before it reached its designated spot.

Generally speaking, camels become pregnant during the winter. That is another reason why the bedouins lead their camels to oases during this season. This is why Sodari ibn Naql ibn Deeb Banu Murra al Taqlib and his group of nomads had arrived at the *wadi* (valley) in the desert.

He kept a close watch on the camel. Should we settle down here permanently? Should we make a home for ourselves like the *hadaris* and provide for a secured life for our future generations? He pondered over the question.

The question, 'how do we provide fodder to the animals if we put down roots at one spot?' bothered him. He also feared that if they did settle down at one spot, he and his kinsmen might become overly attached to worldly possessions just like the rest of the town dwellers. Will his people begin to lay claim to land that his ancestors did not own? His thoughts raced as he walked along.

The desert is not a mere wasteland. It is a treasure trove of ideas. Its impermanence is an enduring lesson to all humans. If we stayed put at one place, would we not relinquish the limitless independence that it offers? No plant or creeper ever puts its roots deep into the desert soil. Isn't this the lesson taught to us by our forefathers as well? The bedouins consider lingering at one place equivalent to a death sentence, and so have never spent too long at one spot. Such prolonged stay invites myriads of problems. How do you fetter a free spirit? A cowardly existence like that, claiming rights over land and soil, would mean invoking a hundred different artifices merely in order to survive. Not just that. To sustain the body, far removed from the spray of the desert sand, and to furbish the new living spaces one would need to adopt several craven material deceits and, as a result, end up demeaning one's life. Was such an existence really called for? There is yet another issue in settling down at one particular spot. We would then need to spend our lifetime safeguarding our possessions. We also entirely lose the capability of raiding travelling caravans during times of dire need. It is not wrong to rob trading parties or farmers when we are desperate to save our own lives. When rains fail, it is this activity that enables us to survive. Similarly, it is the bedouins' duty to provide assistance to those who are lost in the desert, or are our guests. Our forefathers have held that it is not wrong to raid a settlement or rob travellers at times when we ourselves are in danger of losing our lives. Similarly, while it is our primary duty to render assistance to people in trouble, it is no sin to plunder others when the occasion calls for it. It is not wrong to snatch possessions from people who have accumulated more than their fair share of worldly goods. In fact, on occasions it is almost mandatory to do so. Sometimes desert-dwelling *jinns* appear in the form of wayfarers before us. That is why wandering travellers need to be treated with respect and plied with hospitality. If the *jinns* are pleased with our generosity, they will themselves provide us with material things when we find ourselves in dire straits. They may themselves create the opportunity for us to raid caravans. They may themselves appear before us as travelling traders, induce us to rob them, hand over their riches to us, and provide us protection. If we settled down permanently at one spot, the age-old connection with the *jinns* might be snapped forever. The treasure trove of poetry that the *jinns* unlock for our benefit would then dry up and cease altogether. If that happens, how do we transmit to our descendants the knowledge and experience that our ancestors had accumulated? How do we survive without *jinns*? Our generation might also then fail to reach the mysterious and magical land of *Abqer Wadi*.

If we stayed put at one place, we might miss out on the unbounded treasure on offer from the *jinns*. Or else, the opportunity to earn wealth by offering protection to traders might be lost altogether. We are the ones who are aware of every trail in the uncharted sea that is the desert. Just as the birds are familiar with their regular routes across the sky, so are we in the know of the various facets presented by the desert's landscape. Would this unique knowledge not fade away if we decide to settle down at one place? The memory of the desert that is seared in our collective minds might then be lost forever. Our ancestors' practice of singing poems while traversing the desert might also fade from our memories. This method of passing on our forefathers' knowledge to succeeding generations through poems and songs might become extinct and a forgotten art. Our future generations might lose their ability to think for themselves and might end up living like naive town dwellers. A day might come when we may end up simply existing with no perception of the beings that dwell not just in our world but also in the magical realm of the *jinns*. The maximum time we spend at one place is thirty nights. We then start feeling restless. In these circumstances, how can we stay put at one location all our lives? Such a life is unlikely to teach a man any lessons. If we yearn for a comfortable existence, we would end up fearing death. A man who fears death is no bedouin. I do not wish my future generations to be known as the people who cravenly sought refuge from the flaming sun.

No....come what may, we should avoid putting down roots at a single location.

My cousins are wrong. We are fearless warriors who crave independence. We are not cowardly weaklings to settle down at one spot. We should not sacrifice our vigour and vitality by doing so.

But....Sodari....when will your children ever find peace? Isn't that possible only if they stayed put at one spot?

That is true. But, how will they survive a famine or a drought? If they continued to rove the desert they would find the necessary resolve and will to confront such calamities. If they settled down at one spot it is doubtful if they can ever endure such trying conditions. It is the desert that teaches survival techniques to a person. He explores newer and better ways of survival from learning novel strategies by leading a nomadic life. He understands the rationale behind events better. Intuition helps him to delve into the roots of human thoughts and actions. Through this understanding he is able to foresee coming events and take appropriate action. It is the desert that aids in fostering this understanding in men's minds. Every feeling of ours emanates from the soul of the desert. Like the desert, our mental make-up too keeps changing every second of the day. Appreciating this, our ancestors had sharpened every one of their senses. Suspicion, arousal, love, anger - every one of these human emotions owes its birth to the desert. The desert also helps men and women to enjoy their physical relationship to the fullest. It is a special experience to copulate under the light of the full moon. My descendants might never know the pleasure of mating atop a high sand dune, away from prying eyes, drenched in the silvery light of the moon and losing themselves in the pure sensation of prolonged lovemaking while exploring each other's bodies. Like me, my children too must enjoy such sexcapades, and fulfil their bodies' longings.

The unique experience of having sex under the open sky with the desert acting as the floor should not end with my generation. The sound of that intercourse carried by the wind, which, when it enters one's ears, provides a stimulus that cannot be expressed in words, or sung as a composition, is one of life's prime moments. My progeny might never enjoy the pleasure of an erection that occurs when the moonlight flows like milk on a woman's bare breasts and onto their tongues, atop sand dunes that themselves stick up like a woman's bosom. What if they never get to experience the stimulus supplied by camel's milk and the sexual prowess stimulated by the meat of the *dabb* (desert lizard)? What if they simply bypass them, dismissing them as just another root or simply another reptile? Wouldn't they miss out on these rare treasures offered up by the desert? Lovemaking without the vigour provided by the root of the *rabdhin* tree, meat from the *dabb* or camel's milk is no pleasure at all. When all these three enter a man's system, he is totally transformed. The sex that results would bring the very heavens down. How do I describe the sensation of a million stars surrounding us and transporting us to the stratosphere? Whoa, I get a hard-on just imagining the two of us on top of a sand dune, with nothing to hold us back, panting with lust, expelling every bit of pent-up energy, our heartbeats peaking, losing our footing in the sand both of us tumbling down the dune, falling on our backs with our breath being knocked out, then without bothering to brush ourselves off, making her get on her knees, admiring the view from that angle before entering her from behind with the sand still clinging to our bodies.... whoa, it gives me a hard-on just thinking about it! To produce another son, shall we have sex on the third hour of the fourth night of the full moon, when the star rises in the east, after applying a paste of crushed Khozama flowers to her genitals? This method is sure to produce a handsome male child....should we try this? My progeny should get to know all these secrets of procreation.

My descendants must also experience the sensation of floating in midair, touching the moon, unfettered by the earth and the joy of males and females transforming their bodies. The desert would stand by them in such endeavours. With its permanent illusory form, it would constantly stir humans to extraordinary efforts. It would spread itself out like a mattress in valleys such as these and teach humankind how to procreate. It would teach the right days to engage in sexual relations so as to produce new lives. How can we abandon the desert that not only teaches us how to lead our lives but also aids in human conception?

To abandon the *ramla* and settle down in a fertile valley represents fear of death whereas every moment spent in the desert means laughing in its face. It is the expanse of sand that provides man with the resolve and mental strength to fight death every moment of his life. It is a bed of sand that is limitless, spaceless and timeless. If we settled down at one place, we might lose out on the various life lessons it is capable of teaching us. It not only tunes our senses but also expands our cognitive skills.

That is why we term the house as *qabr* and the graveyard as *beit*. But, in the language of the town dwellers, these words convey the exact opposite meanings. It is obvious that there is a wide difference in the speech patterns of the townsfolk and us, nomads. These differences apply to our living styles as well. Looking at their seemingly luxurious lifestyle, our children might decide that it is the right way to go for a peaceful life, and, in the process, lose their spirit. The practice of translating every emotional or physical experience into poetry and thereby transmitting the knowledge gained from it to future generations might be lost forever.

Along with this loss of mental strength, we might also lose out on the physical strength provided by the desert. Every new-born child would lose out on the power it acquires by leaving the protective shade and venturing out into the sun just five days after its birth.

Our body and mind are both nurtured by the desert. Its air strengthens us. It is not easy for us to live away from it.

What should we do?

Sodari returned to where his cousins were pitching their camp. He addressed them, "*Ya walad*, I agree with what you said. To stay put at one spot is insulting to the memory of our ancestors. Let us just stay here till this *sheeta* (winter) ends and proceed to our next destination in spring."

They looked at each other and appeared to be communicating some message via their eyes. This silent signal was not lost on Sodari.

He looked into their eyes and demanded, "Well, what do you say? It is obvious we cannot survive without the desert. So, let's keep moving….as soon as winter ends, we shall look for another suitable location for the camels…. do you agree?"

The eldest among them cleared his throat and ventured, "We have decided to stay put here. If *you* want, you may move on with your children," and raised his head to look Sodari in the eye. The other four echoed the same sentiment.

His sons had a hard time preventing a furious Sodari from engaging in a physical altercation with his cousins. They somehow managed to pull him away and take him back to their tent.

He sat there in silent contemplation. He gazed at the *saqr* (falcon) that his younger son was rearing, like the bedus of the south did. He looked into its fierce eyes and examined its body. Its screech prickled his *shenab* (moustache) and caused his breath to catch. I was right to name this son after my great-grandfather. Like him, he also adores falcons. His lips curved in an involuntary smile. My ancestors have not perished. They have merely stopped their wanderings. That's all. It is now up to us to preserve their thoughts and ideas.

"*Ya walad,* collect all our belongings and let's go. If we have any stuff belonging to them, return it to them before we leave. We shouldn't tarry here a moment longer. *Fehamth ya Rajjaal* (Got it)?"

He made sure his voice was loud enough to be audible to his cousins as well. His thirteen sons immediately placed their right forefingers over their right eyes and acknowledged his instruction, saying, "*Al Haen*!" in one voice.

Sodari's first wife immediately got up, pursed her lips and let out a series of high-pitched trills, accompanied by a rapid back and forth movement of the tongue, known as *zaghrouta* (ululation). Upon hearing this expression of joy, his other three wives and daughters too joined in the noisy celebration, loud enough to rock the entire valley. Some of the menfolk shot arrows in the air and yelled out in support of his decision.

Standing atop a tall sand dune, watching his family approach, Sodari came to a decision. He would split his thirteen sons and four unborn children into two groups with one permanently settling down at one spot while the other continued their nomadic way of life. While each was free to make his own decision in this regard, since he was the one who was well aware of his childrens' capabilities, he decided he would determine which of them would stay where.

The caravan came up to the foot of the hillock and stopped. Sodari came down the sand dune.

We need to find a fertile *wadi* (valley) with adequate water supply. We need to decide which of us will settle there. What if the other dogs come in search of his sons to pick a fight with them? The rest of his kinsmen in the desert should then stand alongside his family in solidarity. No. I'm going about it all wrong. Two of my bravest persons will stay back with my sons at the spot.

Sodari leapt up, propelling himself off the ground, planted his right foot on the camel's side, straightened himself, looped his left leg around the camel's body and landed on its back. He kissed the camel and loudly urged it on with cries of "hath, hath'. As the other camels followed in his wake, the sun's rays fell and spread across the desert. As a few members of the group thought back about crossing the golden-hued sand dunes at dusk, some of them began to sing a dirge about the family members left behind.

As silence enveloped the desert like a mirage, their singing seemed to echo in every direction. As the lines entered his ears, even though they initially provoked anger within him, they still managed to pierce his heart.

The lines evoked memories of his father, uncles and forefathers causing his eyes to mist up and blur his vision of the way ahead.

He began to ponder over ways to etch the poem forever in their memories so that it might not disappear along with the desert wind. Fresh questions began to bother him.

How do I arrange marriage alliances for my sons now that we have antagonised our kinsmen?

"*Akhu noora*", didn't our great-grandfather's grandfather also part from his family members in this fashion? Didn't he survive? Why should you worry? Everything will be fine.....

Sodari kicked the camel's stomach with his left leg. It began to trot.

The women followed, still ululating. Their *khelayaths* (necklaces) and *hujool aw benajil* (bangles) made out of *fudda* (silver) vied with each other as they jangled at every step. A group of five Black slave girls followed the sound of their clanging jewellery.

Is this what we were rushing for, the women thought angrily but covered it up with laughter.

As they climbed down the sand dune, they found their menfolk in an awkward pose and laughingly asked them, "*Ish ya Rajjal?* (What's up, you guys)?"

When they saw their men squatting as though seated on a toilet, the ladies could not control their laughter. The men were squatting and inspecting something on the ground closely. When they heard the women's query, one of them rose and announced, "It appears someone has been buried alive here." When they heard that, the women rushed down the dune.

They then stood to one side and watched as their menfolk pulled the buried men out of the sand, sprinkled water on their faces and gave them water to sip from their waterskins. They wondered among themselves if it was *jinns* pulling a trick on them. From top of the dune a voice was heard, "Are they alive?"

Shocked, the women raised their heads and looked up. It was Sodari seated on his camel at the top of the sand dune. The sight frightened the little girls in the caravan, who thought he was addressing them from the skies and were scared that the *jinns* might get them. They hid behind their mothers and looked around them in fear.

It has been an age-old practice for Sodari to lead and show the way and for the rest of the men and women to follow in his wake. That day, however, something had possessed him and he had raced ahead of all the others and disappeared from their sight. Even though the men following him had urged their camels to follow at full speed, they could find no trace of him. It was while the men were waiting for the womenfolk to catch up with them that they saw him on top of the sand dune exhorting them, "*Ta'al, ya walad*" in his stentorian voice. He urgently instructed his men to quickly run down and dig at a particular spot. They had jumped down from their mounts and hurried to the spot indicated.

As soon as he was informed that there were men buried at that spot, Sodari bent down and withdrew his sword from the scabbard tied to the belly of the camel. Holding it between his teeth, he kicked the camel with his left foot. As though waiting for the signal, the animal turned and, holding its neck back, broke into a canter.

As though reading its master's mind, it ran up a towering sand dune, reached its top and stood there blowing gently.

Sodari's eyes scanned every direction keenly attempting to locate the presence of outsiders. No one was visible. Could it be the work of *jinns*? He now tuned his ears to detect if any foreign sound could be heard. Nothing was perceptible. When he had assured himself that it was indeed the handiwork of *jinns* and came down to the spot, his men had dug up the buried men out of the sand and were slaking their thirst.

Everyone in his entourage was amazed how he had discerned the presence of these men under the sand.

As his camel descended the dune, from his position on the camel, he looked at the foreigners who had been dug out of the sand and asked, "*Min inta* (Where do you come from)? Whose slaves are you?"

Four black forms had emerged from the sand. No one understood their response or the language in which it was spoken. Everyone looked at Sodari.

After a brief pause, Sodari asserted, "These are slaves of the mountain-dwelling Aseer bedouins of southwest Arabia, and they are speaking their language." These words addressed to his people were also meant as a reassurance to himself that these were no *jinns*. Their language was familiar to him as he was proficient in all the dialects spoken by the various bedouin tribes of Arabia. He was also well aware of their cultural differences.

He called out to his third son and instructed him to feed the men honey and goat's milk. The son immediately ran towards the womenfolk. At this, Sodari's first wife muttered loudly enough to be heard by the other wives, "If he goes on feeding every stray found on the way in this manner, we'd be left with nothing to eat but sand."

Her whisper carried to Sodari, who burst out angrily, "Shut up and do as you're told." And, when he saw his second wife's lips twist in a smile at this admonishment, he addressed her in her own dialect of Arabic, "Hey you, my second wife....it seems you're getting very proficient at the art of spying....." and stunned her into silence.

When he saw his son dribbling honey from the container into their mouths, he grew incandescent with rage and shouted, "I'll cut you to pieces....give them the whole pot...."

As though his father's enraged voice had sliced his throat, Sodari's son shuddered, handed the men the honey pot and took one step backwards.

The men took whole handfuls of honey, licked them up and guzzled the goat's milk and sat down exhausted. In the meantime, another of Sodari's sons, a very young Zoubi, ran up to the women, picked up a sack of flour, dropped it in front of the rescued slaves and looked up at his elder brother. The latter's eyes sought his father's, which spat fire.

"You don't even have the sense that little boy possesses. Give them that sack of flour," ordered Sodari who then called the seven-year old Zoubi to come to him. Zoubi skipped as he ran towards his father.

The camel seemed to read Sodari's mind. As Zoubi came running towards him, the camel slowly bent its front legs, folded its body and lowered its back legs as it sat down on the ground. Zoubi put his leg on its haunches and jumped up on its back. Sodari pulled him to the front and hugged him tightly and planted a kiss on his cheek. Overcome by emotion, he kissed Zoubi's head repeatedly. By naming his son after his great-grandfather's great-grandfather, he had wished to immortalise the bedouin tribe called Zoubi, who had once saved the life of one of his ancestors. He had named his son Zoubi so that the bedouin habit of providing succour to the weak and helpless would continue among his descendants also. He was moved to see that his wish was indeed coming true in the form of his son.

As soon as Zoubi was seated, the camel slowly arose - first standing up on its hind legs before extending its front legs. Sodari hugged Zoubi tightly, when he saw the boy was frightened by the animal's ungainly movement. The camel stood quietly. He looked at the group of slaves and asked them who their masters were. He could not decipher their response. Thinking he would be a fool to give up this freebie that had fallen into his lap, he asked them to follow his caravan, urged his camel forward and started on his way once again.

His existing crew of slaves received the newcomers with a mixture of suspicion and affection. They had been bought by Sodari at an auction in Riyadh, a town to the east in the Najd province.

14

Sundar fumbled for words, trying to string together sufficient Arabic to express himself.

"*Kalam* (say something), *ya Sundar*!"

Sundar lifted his head and looked at the speaker. This was the first time he had heard his *kafeel* (sponsor) raise his voice.

"Listen, you're in deep trouble and I'm in no position to help you out. It's entirely your fault. Do one thing: talk to the doctor, he's also an Indian, and then decide what you want to do. *Insha'allah*, everything will turn out all right ...."

Sundar nodded in agreement. His *kafeel* was telling him in simple, comprehensible Arabic to consult the Indian doctor at the hospital, and decide upon the next course of action. It was also clear that he wanted to wash his hands of the problem.

Sundar began planning how to broach the subject to the doctor from Hyderabad.

He waited for the doctor at the rear entrance to the hospital. The doctor put in an appearance an hour later.

Short in stature, with an aquiline nose, wide eyes and curly hair - he began to discuss the case with Sundar in Hindi.

Sundar was a little reassured when the doctor started off by saying he was fully aware of the circumstances of the case. When he mentioned the conclusions contained in the police report, Sundar's face, which had been morose all this while, suddenly acquired a new bloom. He felt an urge to hug the doctor in the manner of Arabs, and plant a kiss on his forehead. Curbing that instinct, he listened to the doctor's words with mounting delight.

"Hospital charges would amount to some thirty thousand. To repatriate the body home would cost another twenty thousand. So, give some thought to my suggestion....if you feel it's not doable, then you better arrange for the required money. You'll need a police clearance after you've settled the hospital bill. Once these are done, you need to book the flight. You'll receive the body only after all these formalities have been completed," said Faisal Ashrafi, the doctor from Hyderabad.

As soon as he drove out of the hospital precincts, Sundar felt as though someone was sawing at his throat with a serrated knife. His stomach roiled. He stopped his car by the side of the road and retched, but nothing came out. He lifted his head and looked up at the sky. Though there were a few scattered stars, the sky appeared barren to him. He took a quick gulp of water from a bottle in the car. As he was on the verge of breaking into tears, the sound of the ringing telephone came as a diversion.

"Hmmm....hmmmm....I'll tell you tomorrow.....I said tomorrow, didn't I? Stupid woman, how many times do I have to repeat myself? Where are you now, bitch? Where? How many times have I told you not to visit them? Didn't I tell you that last night as well? Is he there now? Who? Him.... I need you to get back home before I finish counting to ten....What are you doing there at this time anyway? Isn't it nine-thirty at night there? Didn't I tell you, I'm taking care of things here, and will call whenever I get a chance? So why the fuck are you pestering me now? You simply need an excuse to go to that fellow's house, isn't it? Hang up now, you cunt, and go home...."

After making sure his wife had reached home, he got back into the car. As he inserted the key into the ignition, his cousin Sivaraman came to mind. His ire spiked. Could it be that his wife and Sivaraman were....? Or, was it someone else from the village.....?

He cursed his inability to get on a flight and head for home straightaway.

The neon lights on the street hurt his eyes. He did not feel like going back to his room. He once again stopped the car and thought for a moment about where else he could go.

Yes....that is it....let's go there.....there's no way they could have heard about this matter....spending some time with them might give me a little relief....it might lighten my mood somewhat....

Sundar drove straight to Hussein bhai's *mandi*.

Hussein bhai, originally from Tirunelveli, was famous in that town for preparing and catering *mandi*, an Arabic dish consisting of meat and rice. Having come to Saudi Arabia fifteen years ago, he was the preferred caterer for most Arabian gatherings in town. He would skin a whole lamb, boil it with spices and then slow cook it in a tandoor oven until tender, cover it with mountains of flavoured basmati rice and serve the dish on large salvers. Based on customers' preferences, he would substitute camel, goat or chicken in place of lamb. He employed ten persons in his catering service, all of them from his hometown.

When Sundar had heard, upon his arrival, that a Tamilian was running a successful *mandi* in the town, he had visited the restaurant for the first time on a Friday evening. The visit had reinvigorated him.

Everyone there had showered a lot of warmth and tenderness upon him. An imperceptible feeling of affection had taken root in his heart. Thereafter, whenever he had problems, either back home in India or here with the local Saudis, it had become his habit to unburden himself at the *mandi*.

From their stories he had come to learn of the events that had taken place in the town before his arrival. Since he arrived here, he had never witnessed a single public execution. The last time such an event had taken place in the town, he had been away in India on vacation. He had widely expressed his bitter disappointment at having missed out on that awesome spectacle of a man beheading another. He kept imagining how it must have felt from the accounts related to him by various friends. He had also shivered with fright at nights at some of the gory tales related to him by Hussein *bhai*'s men at the *mandi*. It had also become his habit to retail such stories during his telephone conversations to India with his own embellishments. One such story was that of the two Indians and the two Pakistanis.

One of the regulars at Hussein *bhai*'s *mandi* was the Saudi, Sulaiman ibn Ahmed al Saaqi, a *hadari*. He had a very fair complexion, which immediately identified him as a *hadari, and* set him apart from bedouins who were normally brown-skinned. It was also usual for most Indians to get confused when confronted with fair-skinned bedouins. But, for experienced people like Hussein *bhai*, it was easy to guess whether a person was a bedouin or a *hadari* from his speech and mannerisms. To most Indians, however, an Arab was an Arab. There have been many who had lived in Saudi Arabia for thirty years or more without getting to know the basic differences between a bedouin and a *hadari*.

Sulaiman ibn Ahmed al Saaqi only resembled a *hadari* in looks. His speech, comportment and fearless nature were all totally that of a bedouin. Some people even laughed behind his back at his attempts to act like a bedouin. It was widely rumoured that his great-grandfather had migrated from this town to Dammam in Sharqiyah province over a hundred years ago. His grandfather, in an attempt to show they were bedouins and not *hadaris*, had returned to this town in Najd province in an attempt to assimilate with the local bedouins. But, unfortunately for him, none of the Sheikhs belonging to any of the *faqats* (clans) of the Sodari *kabeela* (tribe) were willing to accept him as one of their own. Having failed to establish himself here as a bedouin, he had gone back to Sharqiyah. He managed to educate his children well and set them up in prestigious government positions. Some, he trained to become religious scholars, and thus gain status in society. A few others joined the Saudi armed forces. They not only fought the wars in Yemen and Israel but had also been part of the forces that successfully raised the siege on Mecca. Three of his sons had played a big part in the operation against the Iranian demonstrators who clashed with Saudi security forces at Islam's holiest city.

Having established all his sons in their respective careers, he decided it was time to return to his roots and spend his last few years at the place of his ancestors. His fifth son, Ahmed ibn Mubarak al Saaqi accompanied him to Sulayyil in the Najd province and set him up with a house and a fifteen acre *mazra* (farm). The government at that time was assisting the nomadic bedus to settle down by offering them free land near towns and financial assistance to pursue agriculture. But many among them, unwilling to settle down, would sell their holdings, buy camels with the money and wander off into the trackless desert once again. Sulaiman's father, Ahmed ibn Mubarak al Saaqi had bought his land from one such group of bedouins, carried out agricultural activities and, in course of time, had become one of the richest men in the area. He grew a grass variety known as *berseem,* and supplied it to traders who sold it not only within the Najd and Sharqiyah provinces but also exported it abroad. In the process he soon attained the status of a prominent businessman. He had come to live in the area only in deference to his father's wishes and never gave a second thought to the fact that the bedouins did not accept him as one of their own. But Sulaiman, on the other hand, strained every sinew to achieve his grandfather's unfulfilled wish.

In order to achieve the social status of a bedouin, he used to move closely with certain *faqats* (clans) of the Sodari *kabeela* (tribe). He believed that, given his wealth and financial status, they would accept him as a bedouin sooner or later. Having heard of several such instances in the past, he was also hoping to establish a blood relationship with the bedouins. He preferred the company of bedouins not only during *eid* festivities but also at his regular get-togethers at home. He nursed the ambition of marrying a bedouin girl one day, but kept that aspiration hidden deeply within his heart. When that yearning went up in smoke one day, he had gone berserk. It was then that he was chopped into several pieces and dumped into a borewell by the two Indians and two Pakistanis.

A close *hadari* friend of Sulaiman ibn Ahmed al Saaqi, Ahmed ibn Rashid, had eloped with Hind, a girl belonging to the Arrakumeem *faqat* of the Sodari *kabeela*. The news spread like wildfire and Sulaiman was deeply shaken by the violent reaction, not only from the girl's own *faqat* but also from youngsters belonging to various other *faqats* who, via their telephone chats and messages, were seen baying for the couple's blood. They wanted to hunt the duo down and kill them to avenge their *kabeela*'s honour. When he heard the news, Sulaiman was frightened to his core and saw his dreams turn to ashes in front of his eyes. Several bedouins, who considered the *hadari*'s act as an insult to their clan, also cut off their relationship with Sulaiman. Not having expected such a violent backlash, an angry and upset Sulaiman left for his *mazra* hoping to unwind there.

Two Indians - Mohammed from Virudhachalam and Shakibur Rahman from Bihar - and two Pakistanis - Wasimullah and Muneer from Peshawar - were employed at his *mazra*. It was common knowledge that Sulaiman used to routinely mistreat these four. While curses and beatings were commonplace, the abuse also extended to withholding their wages and preventing them from travelling back to their homes. Once, while bemoaning their fate, the four of them jointly decided to teach Sulaiman a lesson if and when an opportunity presented itself. But they perhaps did not envisage that their decision would have such far-reaching consequences and end up disrupting their own lives.

Sulaiman was under great mental tension that day due to the *hadari*-bedouin confrontation. As soon as he parked his Land Cruiser and saw the Bihari workman taking a breather between chores, he picked up an iron rod that was lying nearby, ran up to Shakib and began abusing and laying about him indiscriminately in blind rage. The other three workers, who observed this, came running to save their compatriot. The two Pakistanis attacked Sulaiman and pushed him to the ground, and all the four then beat him up mercilessly.

After having exhausted all their pent-up anger, the four workers took a short rest. Shakib then got up, went to where Sulaiman lay bleeding on the ground, and taking hold of the injured man's jaw with his left hand, shook him. At that, Sulaiman quickly got up and started running towards his vehicle. That move stunned the four men who quickly realised he was going for his pistol in the jeep. Muneer yelled out, "Stop him….don't let him get his gun….catch him…." and, rushing into his quarters, quickly came out with a machete. In the meantime, the other three subdued Sulaiman and pinned him to the ground. Pushing them aside, Muneer plunged the machete straight into Sulaiman's chest. Blood spurted out and the sight of it seemed to push the assailant over the edge. Muneer pulled the machete out of Sulaiman's chest and began hacking at his throat.

Once all the noise, fight and anger subsided, the four of them chopped Sulaiman's body into pieces, stuffed them into a sack and dropped it into a borewell.

The news only came out several months later when the water from the well began to run red. The police arrested the four men and, in due course, they were publicly beheaded at the town square.

It was to listen to such thrilling stories that Sundar used to visit Hussein *bhai*'s *mandi*. Having been deprived of the opportunity of witnessing them firsthand himself, he would secretly rehash them and relish these tales. Hundreds of opportunities have since presented themselves for Sundar to visit the *mandi*, which was the fountainhead for many such stories for him. It was also more usual for him to drop in there on occasions when he was down in the dumps and needed his spirits lifted.

That is why Sundar was now proceeding towards Hussein *bhai*'s *mandi*. He had not been there since the day the problem with Rajendran had first raised its head. Reassuring himself that they could not possibly know of the enormous proportions the issue had ballooned into, he decided to head there to find some solace. He firmly believed that the place offered him peace of mind.

But the moment he entered the place, Razak, one of the workers there, asked him, "What's this I hear, Sundar *anna*? I believe someone committed suicide by hanging himself in your quarters. Is it true? Who was it?"

Sundar stood there stunned. He exhaled loudly and tried to give them a plausible explanation.

"It's my cousin, *anna*....what to do....he had no patience.....he stole some money from some of the boys in the room and also from Ahmed *bhai*'s laundry. Our boys demanded it back....they also telephoned home and informed his mother....his mother probably questioned him about it....and, out of shame, he hanged himself. While he's gone now, it's me who's left holding the bag .... I'm now stuck with a hundred and one problems....you know very well what the police here are like.....a thousand questions.....an enquiry....as though it was I who strung him up ....somehow all the formalities are now complete. But the body needs to be sent back home and that's what is worrying me now.....apparently, it'll cost fifty thousand riyals! Where do I go for such a large sum of money? As soon as I inform his parents, his father will immediately launch a campaign against me claiming it was I who killed his son....I'm totally lost and don't know what to do next...."

While returning to his room, with the two thousand riyals donated by Hussein *bhai*, Rajendran appeared before his mind's eye. He could hear Rajensdran's voice clearly in his ears. Memories of both of them travelling together for their work in the same car came flooding back, and, for a moment, he felt scared.

As uncontrollable sobs broke out, he quickly stopped the car, pressed his forehead against the steering wheel and wept loudly. Fear of the unknown overcame him once again.

He stopped crying and began to think rationally. He needed to decide quickly on the Hyderabadi doctor's proposal. Every time he thought about it, a picture of a whole sheep being roasted in the tandoor at Hussein *bhai*'s restaurant kept entering his mind. He took a deep breath, composed himself, considered his decision carefully and, selecting his words cautiously, called the doctor:

"Hello, doctor....*Salam Alaikum*....how are you? Yes, I agree we'll proceed as you suggested....you may take any organ you want from the body....yes, yes....I've spoken to his father and obtained his consent....they can't afford to repatriate the body to India spending such a lot of money, doctor....that's why....okay....yes, they have agreed you may remove eyes, liver, kidney and any other organ you require.....we'll use that money to send the body back home.... there's no other go, doctor....they say he can't be buried here because he's a non-Muslim.... so the body needs to be sent back to India....yes, doctor....okay sir....I'll come around in the morning and sign the necessary papers....if needed, I can come over there now itself...huh? Okay, I'll come there right now, doctor....*shukran....shukran jazilan* (thank you very much)...."

He sighed and drove towards the hospital.

Very soon, an image of his wife's breasts came up before his eyes. He held her fleshy thighs tight and thrust his hip forward, while pressing hard on her big toe. Her body began to gyrate of its own accord.

15

Dheeb ibn Hrar ibn Jassas ibn Murra ibn Khulaif Taqlib Ar Rabiya halted his camel under the shade of a tree, to provide his mount a little respite, and dismounted from its back. He took a drink of water from a waterskin and gave some to the camel as well. He then made it kneel on the ground and sat down himself.

The sun was about to rise. He saluted the mountain that was visible ahead, hailing it in his mind as the sacred Tuwaiq Mountain, their ancestral goddess. This was new terrain as far as he was concerned. He had never been to this stretch of the desert before. He had started out in search of a new location in which to pitch camp before the next rains. In his ten years' experience of leading his bedouin camel train to fresh pastures, this was the first time he had come across this particular spot. It was a valley surrounded on all sides by mountains. He could see that the soil there was rich and fertile. Years of rainwater seeping into the soil had nourished it, allowing lush green grass to grow in abundance. He stood up and surveyed the area as far as his eyes could see. The mountain appeared to be quite distant from where he stood. He decided then and there that this is where members of his *kabeela* would settle down permanently.

He got up and started to pace while reciting a *qasida*. He stopped abruptly.

Wow! Wonderful ... .oh, my goddess of the mountain ... .what a beautiful poem you've blessed me with ... oh! I wish I hadn't run out of wine.....if I had some more, I could develop the theme even better ... .no, I shouldn't let the idea disappear.... I will reshape it in an even better form and recite it at this year's festival for the goddess in Makkah and surpass the greatness of Imru al-Qais, Abu Al Marri and all the other great bards. My lines should also be etched in letters of gold on the walls of the temple of the goddess in Makkah. My poem is no less worthy than the al Mu'allaqat compositions..... listen, oh world, there are people in my *kabeela* too who are capable of composing poetry that would rock the world....

Dheeb ibn Hrar ibn Jassas ibn Murra ibn Khulaif Taqlib Ar Rabiya jumped about in elation.... I'll see you all at this year's poetry competition.... I've just thought of a composition that no other bedouin group can even visualise.... Did you think we were thickheaded oafs? You, the slutty al-Birra bedouins.... It's your habit to put on airs for no good reason.... Let's see what transpires this year.... It'll be a showdown between you and us.... This year our *kabeela* will surely recapture the crown that was snatched from us a few years back.... I swear this on my great-grandfather Murra.... Did you think the al Taqlibs are to be taken lightly? Did you think our only pastime was to whore around in a constant state of drunkenness? Sons of bitches! Come and confront us if you dare at the poetry competition in this year's festival....

Dheeb ibn Hrar Taqlib Ar Rabiya suddenly paused. Something struck him and he looked around keenly. Is someone following me....he sharpened his ears and placed his hand on the hilt of the *jambiya* on his waist. He looked all around carefully. No one was visible. But how is it that he heard someone breathing? Could it be a *jinn*?

He walked ahead with eyes at the back of his head. He had hardly progressed two feet when realisation struck him that there was apparently some affinity between this land and his poetry. Is this sacred soil? He drew in a long breath. Is this where the goddess Manat was born….. or is it land that had been blessed by her?

My goddess, Tuwaiq! What kind of a miracle is this? Why did a poem that I had never thought of before in my life suddenly strike me here? Tell me … ..oh mother … .I hereby swear to you that if my poem wins this year's Makkah poetry competition, I will not kill my next child if it turns out to be a girl…. Yes, my goddess, I make this solemn vow to you….if the child that's due to me next turns out to be a girl, I'll not sacrifice her to you……instead, I'll name her after you and cherish her for having blessed me with such a wonderful composition….

There is someone else around here. Without the shadow of a doubt.

Could this have been the capital of the kingdom of Kindha? Wasn't Imru al-Qais a prince of Kindha? Could this be the place where he grew up? He was one of the emperors of ancient Arabic poetry. He led a completely hedonistic life filled with wine, women and song, and wrote earth-shattering poetry. No one could hope to match his compositions. My god! What a poet he was! Even while the sand dunes kept shifting their shapes and locations, he could accurately identify the locations where he composed each of his verses. He could also unerringly name the women he had sex with while composing every one of his verses. Arabic took on a new brilliance in his works; the language was rejuvenated and acquired a special fragrance in his hands. His riddles and posers were exceptional. To this day, no one had beaten him at versification; it was unlikely that anyone would in the future either. Such had been his greatness. That is why his lines are etched in letters of gold on the walls of the goddess' temple at Makkah.

My poems should also be spoken of in the same breath as his compositions.... My lines should also find a place on those sacred walls.... That will happen only if my verse is judged as being better than the seven al Mu'allaqat poems. Further, the poem needs to be approved by the heads of all the bedouin tribes. How likely is that? It is no easy feat to achieve. The judges are experts and well-versed in Arabic poetry.

Not only that, times have changed considerably. There is a lot of personal animosity between bedus. If one of them approves my composition, there will be ten others to oppose the move. Come what may, I'm determined to win this time.

Dheeb ibn Hrar Taqlib Ar Rabiya turned back. The camel stood up as though anticipating his return. It affectionately licked the top of his head with its tongue. In turn he stroked its long, droopy *kasham* (nose) lovingly and kissed its muzzle. He was among those bedouins who believed that the pride, strength and beauty of a camel lay in its nose. He then massaged its legs and gave it some fodder out of a bag. As it chomped on the leaves, huffing with pleasure, he again heard sounds of human breathing. He withdrew the *jambiya* from its scabbard at his waist, held it in his left hand, quickly slid his *saif* (sword) from its place at the camel's underbelly, and holding it in his right hand, asked in a loud tone, "*Meen? Meen adha* (who is it)?"

Stroking the camel's belly, he cast his eyes all around. No one was visible. But the soft sound of human breathing was coming from somewhere. He cocked his ears and listened to where the sound was coming from.

It didn't seem to come from the ground level. He looked up. There appeared to be someone up on the tree. He tugged the camel forward and circled the tree cautiously. He cast his eyes all around and searched among the branches. He was certain there was something among the branches. Could it be an animal of some kind? The *jambiya* now shifted to his right hand and the *saif* to the left.

He looked at the camel. It chewed its cud and looked back at him, slowly raising its neck. He was well aware that along with speed, the animal also possessed calmness and tranquillity. But today, that calmness appeared to him to be out of the ordinary. Suddenly, the camel's measured gait and calm appearance seemed to produce an unusual feeling within him and provide his feet with a sense of security.

Pacing around softly, he scrutinised the branches of the tree carefully.... it was a human being.... There! He could see two eyes staring back at him..... It looked like a young girl....

"*Enzil, ya bint* (get down, you girl)," he said and looked around. No one else was visible. No sound could be heard apart from the sibilant hiss of the girl's breathing. He inhaled the wind and analysed its scent. No other human smell was discernible. He looked up again at the tree. He suddenly grew irate.

"Come down, girl," he yelled in irritation this time.

Immediately, a young girl jumped down from the tree. He grew a little alarmed. Could it be a *jinn*? Had it appeared in a human form to harm him or to present him with the gift of poetry? Could this place be the fabled *Abqer Wadi*?

He scrutinised her carefully. Even though her appearance suggested she was scared, he could fathom that her eyes held fire.

"*Meen inthi* (Who're you)?" he asked.

Instead of replying, the youngster started running. He went after her, caught hold of her and reassured her with these words, 'there's no need to fear. I am the head of a bedouin group from the north. I uphold the bedouin tradition of assisting those in trouble. My ancestors have taught me that I should stand by that person and protect him even if he happens to be my enemy. Look, you can trust me. Here, take my sword and dagger.... Cut off my head if I so much as look at you askance ... .I am an al Taqlib bedu of the ar-Rabiya lineage who considers his word worth more than his life....'

The maiden stood looking at him for a few moments and then, in one leap, jumped onto the back of his camel and sat astride it. He stood there stunned. I have never seen a remarkable person like her before. Even men struggle to mount a camel in that fashion! She must surely be a *jinn* enchantress.

The camel carried both of them securely coasting over the desert's undulating sand dunes. Three other beautiful camels accompanied them. Once he had reassured himself, through the medium of her body heat, that she was indeed of human extraction, he kissed the crown of her head. She took hold of his hands and clutched them protectively around her soft bosom.

Once they reached the place where his *kabeela* was camped, Dheeb ibn Hrar ibn Jassas ibn Murra ibn Khulaif Taqlib Ar Rabiya addressed his tribesmen thus:

"Listen well, pre-eminent scions of the Al Taqlib bedouin tribe, it's up to you to believe me or not, but what I am about to say is the absolute truth. This bedouin girl belongs to the al Zoubi tribe from the south. Her *kabeela* consisted of over three hundred members who owned over two thousand camels and four thousand sheep. There is nothing in the world to equal their al Zoubi camels. Another tribe from the west, let's not name them, coveted their camel herd. But the al Zoubis refused to part with them.

"They maintained that they were the only ones in the world equipped to handle the camels, but the western bedouins had been persistent in their demand. As the argument escalated and grew heated, the al Zoubis had killed two of the men belonging to the other tribe. The remaining three others, who managed to escape with their lives, returned with a large force. You all know the strength of the western bedus. Over a thousand of them came on horses and camels to wage war. As arrows and spears flew, the defiant al Zoubis, determined not to hand over their camels to the western tribe, packed off their animals in the custody of a hundred women and ten men to escape to an unknown destination. The western tribesmen slaughtered the remaining two hundred al Zoubis, located their hidden camels, killed everyone in this girl's group and carried off their camels. This youngster somehow managed to escape with three of her prized possessions. She survived by staying up on trees at nights. Let us provide her shelter among us and look after her. When she comes of age, we shall marry her off to someone suitable from our own *kabeela*. Should the western bedouin group come here looking for her, we shall stand with her and protect her. I am of the opinion that it is our duty to defend someone who has lost her entire tribe for the sake of a camel. Apart from that, this may also be the right opportunity to put an end once and for all to the arrogance of those western tribesmen. We need to vanquish them and establish permanent peace in the land. Otherwise, they wouldn't hesitate to eliminate us, just as they did with this girl's *kabeela*. Let's have a conclave when we go to Makkah this year for our goddess' festival. We'll try to unite all the bedouins who come there and form a common front against the western bedus. What do you say? Do you agree? Oh, and one more thing....the poetry prize this year is ours! I've composed a wonderful verse.... Come let's expand it further together. Let's compete on its basis, keeping Imru al-Qais' compositions as the benchmark. Are you in agreement? Oh, I forgot....I've brought along three of the wonderful al Zoubi camels and have stabled them nearby. Beautiful animals....of a kind you've never seen before in your lives ....you'd be astounded at their mere sight...."

Dheeb ibn Hrar ibn Jassas ibn Murra ibn Khulaif Taqlib Ar Rabiya expelled a long breath and sat down. It didn't matter if he was ostracised, but he needed to save this girl at all costs. She owns three of the most extraordinary camels in the world. They are no less than wonders of the world. If nobody amongst us comes forward to accept her as his wife, I'll take her myself to be my fourth wife. I'll then start a new clan, separate from this *kabeela*, named al Zoubi al Taqlib, after these marvellous camels.

But the new al Zoubi *kabeela* that he planned did not come into effect immediately. It took several centuries to materialise.

Since Dheeb ibn Hrar Taqlib Ar Rabiya won the poetry contest at Makkah during the festival of the bedouin goddess, before the advent of Islam, he was accepted as one of their own by the al Taqlib tribesmen. Because no one else came forward to marry the girl he had brought with him, he himself took her as his fourth wife. It was only after some fifteen or so generations of their lineage that a separate al Zoubi *faqat* came into existence within the al Sodari *kabeela*. A thousand years before this took place, Umru ibn Murra ibn Hrar Taqlib Ar Rabiya, the great-grandson of Dheeb ibn Hrar Taqlib Ar Rabiya and his fourth wife, had turned out to be a versatile poet.

Umru was planning to obtain an idol of Manat from the bedouin groups who considered her their ancestral goddess and install it at the spot where his great-grandfather had received his inspiration for the poem that had won him that year's Makkah poetry prize. That was the time when the bedouins of the Najd area had switched from venerating mountains and trees to worshipping idols. People of this region had no way of knowing that a revolutionary change was sweeping other parts of Arabia, and that methods of worship were changing dramatically. The convulsion reached them just as the arrangements for the al Manat festival were gathering steam.

One hundred and fifty camels and three hundred sheep were lined up for slaughter at the festival. Heaps of fruits and mountains of dates were laid out, and a whole well had been filled with wine. The festival attracted not only those bedouins who believed in the goddess Manat but also some of the other tribes. The place was crowded with poets, singers and dancers, while ladies of pleasure added glamour to the gathering.

The bustling arena gave the appearance of heaven on earth. Umru ibn Murra ibn Hrar Taqlib Ar Rabiya was bustling around busily overseeing the arrangements when the heart-wrenching news reached him.

He was informed that a new group had emerged a few years ago in Makkah that opposed idol worship and spoke vehemently against the gods that the bedus venerated.

It was said that they rejected the violent ways of the bedouins and wished to establish a rule based on the principles of peace and harmony. They were totally against the practice of idol worship. In addition, the group was striving to eliminate some of the other unsavoury features of bedouin life such as conceit, violence, drunkenness, lust, female infanticide and poems that glorified these aspects. It aimed at creating a true faith and establishing a peaceful world order. When Umru ibn Hrar Taqlib Ar Rabiya learnt that they had declared a war to eradicate the hundreds of different bedouin deities, and bring everyone under the fold of a single form of worship, he became very perturbed.

More than the fact that the celebrations he had organised were unlikely to take place, he could not accept the reality that the goddess' idol was likely to be smashed to pieces before his very eyes. Thoughts of the special ten-line verses he had composed for the grand occasion, the wine likely to remain stagnant in the well and the untasted charms of the courtesans afflicted him greatly.

He looked around him. Men were scattering in every direction. Camels and sheep were wandering around aimlessly. The platform on which the al Manat idol was to be installed lay bare. He felt like crying at the complete waste.

He was shattered to learn that some of his own cousins had switched to the new religion, having come to the conclusion that peace and conciliation as laid down in the new religion were the only true paths. At the same time, he was also pleased to learn that some bedus, unwilling to give up their old ways or their idols, had decided to fight back against the new religion.

He contemplated his own options.

The ideas preached by the new religion are true to some extent. Our lives which are governed by liquor, excess and blood lust need some moderation. Peace and tranquillity are indeed the need of the hour .... but....

Should we then give up our gods that have been worshipped for centuries from the time of our ancestors? If we did so, wouldn't it be akin to insulting our forefathers? ....He was conflicted.

Finally Umru ibn Murra Taqlib Ar Rabiya came to a conclusion.

This al Manat goddess who bestowed the gift of poetry on my great-grandfather should be protected against any harm.

I shall safeguard her with my own life.

He picked up the majestic, sword-wielding al Manat idol in his hand, mounted his horse and urged it forward.

Umru ibn Murra ibn Hrar ibn Dheeb ibn Hrar ibn Jassas ibn Murra ibn Khulaif Taqlib Ar Rabiya spurred his horse. It shot ahead.

Suddenly he was reminded of his daughter, Hind. And of his wife. She'll be all right. She had another husband to take care of her. But what about Hind?

The al Manat idol strapped to his back was throbbing to his heartbeats.

The horse negotiated a mountain and began descending it.

The vast expanse of the desert. Soft sand that made locomotion difficult. The horse went on its way relentlessly.

He came across an oasis. He stopped there for a short rest. He let the horse drink and had some water himself. He massaged the horse's legs and sprinkled some water over it. He washed his face and sat down for a while. He unstrapped the idol from his back and laid it down on the ground.

He gazed unblinkingly at the pond and the adjoining tree for a while. He then shook himself and stared again with wide-eyed surprise.

Could this be 'that' pond? The place where the prince of Arabic poetry, Imru al-Qais, had a tryst with his love, Unaiza? Did he compose that poem at this very spot?

Imru al-Qais had loved his betrothed Unaiza more than life itself. Even though he had had many affairs with several different women, Unaiza was the one true love of his life.

His poems are a treasure trove of beauty. A prince belonging to the Kindha dynasty, he gave up his royal lifestyle to mingle with commoners, live freely in the open desert, and lead a pleasurable life filled with drinking and chasing women, while being considered the father of Arabic poetry. I need to justify my being named after him by composing a peerless verse in his honour.

When he came to meet his love, Unaiza and found her bathing in a pool with her friends, Imru is said to have snatched up their clothes and climbed up a tree. Could this have been that tree?

When the girls pleaded for their clothes to be returned, the great poet is supposed to have said, "I want you to climb out one by one and I shall return your dresses to you."

Our poet did not pay any heed to their tearful entreaties. Finally, the girls had no option but to get out of the pool one by one. As he handed over their clothes to the other girls, Imru was eagerly looking forward to glimpsing his dream girl Unaiza's unclad form. She baulked at having to come out of the water. Her friends kept urging her, "Come on, Unaiza, come out ... .there's no other option….." while our poet kept smiling smugly at her plight.

Finally, with her eyes closed firmly, she stepped out of the pool shyly. Amazed at the sight of her beautiful nude body, Imru could have temporarily lost his power of versification. His famed eloquence must have deserted him momentarily. Who knows what mental lines he was limning in his own mind with limitless colours in a shower of honey?

He carefully stored the memory of her bewitching body from all angles. As he saw her limbs sliding once again into her dress, he must have thought his entire world was crumbling..

Unable to bear the sight of his dream girl shedding tears of mortification, he slaughtered his most favourite camel and offered it to the girls for their meal.

Subsequently, Imru al-Qais married Unaiza, gave up poetry, wine and extra-marital sex to lead an exemplary life. History also evidences that he then fought his clansmen, who had murdered his father in a battle for succession, and recaptured the throne of Kindha.

Could this be the spot where that history began?

The moon was reflected in Umru ibn Murra al Taqlib's eyes as he proceeded further.

The moonlight that bathed the night's long stretch reminded him of Laila.

Her real name was not Laila, but all Arabic poets name their favourite heroines either Laila or Hind.

She was the epitome of beauty. Her eyes contained the strength of a sandstorm. Her fingers resembled the camel's tongue....

Last month, while dining at a cousin's house, I inadvertently picked up a lamb's tongue. The convention was if anyone came across a lamb's or a camel's tongue in a dish, he must immediately follow it with a verse.

That's when I sang about her. Everyone who heard the composition was so thrilled they expressed a desire to have sex with her at least once....

I wonder where that beautiful nymph was now ... .just a glimpse of her would make a person rampant like a stallion ... .how can I forget the time when my tongue played a symphony on her niples.....She was most probably from Persia, otherwise how would she know about the poet, Abu Nuwas?

To the poets from Najd, who were totally unaware of a place called Baghdad, it was she who described the charms of that city. She was a girl who came down from the skies to write poetry and to inspire poets. I need to write an explosive composition using her nipples as a quill. Under the new dispensation, girls such as her might find no place. Their compositions and the pleasure they dispense might disappear forever. I need to compose a nostalgic tribute in her memory.

It was on a full moon night such as this when I had gone to her for the fourth time. That was when she introduced me to the verses of that wonderful poet named Abu Nuwas. He was also an eccentric person who preferred boys to girls for sexual gratification. His compositions about wine and the pleasures of drink are unparalleled in this world.

My goddess Manat..... you wonderful mother, who blessed my great-grandfather with the gift of poetry..... You need to listen to a composition of Abu Nuwas..... The one that Laila recited to me is still sweet and fresh like honey in my heart.... My great-grandfather, who wrote poetry that could upend this world! You should hear it too.... It's an extraordinary composition from Abu Nuwas, a poet born to an Iranian mother and an Arab father.... He was an eccentric prince of Arabic poetry.... Mother Al Manat, please provide me with the inspiration to produce a verse that is equal to his compositions...... no one should have composed a better poem about lust than me.... Please bestow such a gift upon me, just as you did to my great-grandfather..... My mother Manat, here is Abu Nuwas' poem..... Listen to it first......

Come my sweet cup-bearer, pour me a drink,
Confirm that this wine is of high quality vintage.
There's no need to pour it in secrecy; everything is acceptable here.
Don't spare even a drop for those who drink in secret or to posture.
As far as I'm concerned, pretence is obnoxious.
If there's one thing that promotes good life, it's wine.
So drink up, and even time will bow down before you.
Wine will rejuvenate you.
Saying this doesn't make me a good person, I know my friend,
I'm a total fraud.
Forget that, friend.... Tell me your lover's name
Compose some lines about her that'll cause the listener to envy you.
No, don't cry, my friends.... Do not cry....
Stop pining for your Hinds and Lailas.....
Drink up.... This is the finest distilling of roses!
It'll coat our dry, parched throats like honey.
It'll redden your eyes and cheeks
This wine is the essence of rubies.....
The goblet is made of the finest pearl nacre.
This beauteous female serves you the ruby red wine
In a pearl chalice with her own slender hands.
She's a magical being
Who serves the wine in two ways -

With her hands and through her eyes.
My friends have experienced only one form
Whereas I've enjoyed both!
Look at her, the cup-bearer,
She has also a string of girls
Go with any of them you desire.
I, on the other hand, didn't like any of her girls.
When I first came here the other day,
She asked, "Who knocks on my door at this hour?"
"It's us, a group of ordinary folk,
In need of wine and women,
Open the door…."
"You reject every one of the girls,
Here's a pretty boy, shining like a gold coin
As handsome as the moon, capable of bringing orgasms
To everyone who sleeps with him,
What do you say?" she asked as though reading our mind.
We replied, "Bring him forth straightaway,
We can wait no longer."
She produced him before us
He, with eyes as sparkling as the stars.
You would imagine that a magical time then ensued….
But, no my friends….
He wasn't as pretty as the moon in the sky
One after another we had sex with him throughout that night.
God was looking on
At the sins of our wicked group.
Do not consider this mere braggadocio….

So goes Abu Nuwas' poem.

Oh my mother goddess! Such poems would have no place in the coming times. Wine, lust and poetry might all become taboo under the tenets of the new religion. They may even be forbidden totally. Worship of idols such as yours might disappear from this land forever.

But, I shall protect you. However true their stand might be, I shall still safeguard you - the goddess who gave the gift of poetry to my great-grandfather - with my life, if need be.

Umru ibn Murra ibn Hrar Taqlib Ar Rabiya stopped his horse and dismounted.

A strong wind began blowing. The sand dunes began to shift shape slowly in the wind. The *obaar*, which seemed to span the sky and the earth, rocked Umru and his horse on their feet.

As man and beast floundered in the face of the heavy wind, a group of bedouins were seen making their steady way towards them.

By the time the wind died down, the group had reached where Umru ibn Murra stood. As he shook with fear, they smilingly greeted him saying, "Arhab". Having reassured himself that this was just a band of nomadic bedouins, he responded to their greeting, "Al Bega," while mentally fingering his *jambiya* in case they were highway robbers. He then spoke to them at length while mentally assessing their intentions. He also slowly unfolded the reason for his hurried rush.

They eyed the Al Manat idol curiously. "What's this? Why should anyone seek to break this to pieces? It's just a stone image after all...." they laughingly asked.

Umru ibn Murra grew highly incensed at this ingenuous query. "This is our god ... .it won't be apparent to a brainless heathen group such as yourselves ... .begone from here," he snarled.

The group, unfazed by his reaction, merely laughed and commented, "Sorry, but we do not understand any of your gods," and began wending their way eastwards. The language they spoke among themselves sounded strange to him. He did not understand a single word of it. Was it the

Nabati tongue that was in vogue before Arabic made its appearance? Could it be Roma? Or was the nomadic group speaking the language of our ancestors? Was it the speech that was in force when Arabic parted ways with Nabati? Staring after them for a while, Umru ibn Murra Taqlib fastened the al Manat idol to his chest, mounted the horse and sped towards the south. As he raced on his way, suddenly thoughts about *jinns* struck him.

The *jinns* of poetry avoid me. Can I not write poetry if they refuse to enter me? It is said that my great-grandfather had once defeated even the *jinns* in a poetry contest. That is why they are not well-disposed towards our *kabeela*. A story is prevalent among our group that it was the *jinns* who had killed my great-grandfather in retaliation for his conviction that he did not need them for composing great poetry. But I don't believe it ... .I'm certain it was his own cousins who assassinated him… they killed him for having married a prostitute, and conveniently shifted the blame onto the *jinns*. And here I am, not having extracted revenge for his killing….*Akhu Noora*….turn the horse around….where's that intoxicating herb? Stop, hey, stop….. let's get high first….you, horse…. so you want some too, eh? Here, take it….. I need to be at the bastards' place in the twinkling of an eye…. Got it? My first order of business is to kill them all…. This Al Manat cunt can wait….I need to first kill those cowardly sons of bitches who murdered my great-grandfather…. Fly, fly like the wind…. You'll get as high as a kite….run…..I'm feeling the effect too….. oh, oh, oh my gosh….here's a *jinn* twat….come here, you bitch….I was unnecessarily upset with you….is that why you refused to enter into me? Come, let's go and kill them all together ... .we'll slaughter them to the last man ... .but, wait a minute, weren't you with them all this while? What? They turfed you out after they converted to the new religion? Then, come with me ... .let's join forces and root them out….together we'll initiate a bloodbath….enter into my body and let's compose poetry more wonderful than that of Imru al-Qais…. Fly, you son of a fucking filly….fly….

The horse flew. The *jinn* was seated behind Umru ibn Murra holding on to his waist tightly. The sword-wielding Al Manat idol was attached firmly to his chest. The shocked skies reacted to their frenzied rush with resounding thunder and lightning. The horse's gallop set up an *obaar* that made the sand dunes float in midair.

Standing on his stirrups, Umru ibn Murra Taqlib slashed through the oncoming thunder and lightning and the sand dunes with his sword. A lightning bolt suddenly struck before the oncoming horse and cleaved the ground in front of it into two. The horse stumbled and fell into the crater. The swirling wind gathered up the *jinn* and took it away floating into the sky. Umru raised the fallen horse, remounted it and proceeded on his way once again - but this time, underground. The al Manat idol still clung to his chest.

16

"Just wait....I'll chop him to pieces as soon as he steps out of the airport.....and, you....you old bag, stop spouting stuff like he's my nephew, your first grandson, and so on, or you'll die first by my hands, so help me god ...."

Letting loose this tirade against his mother, Rengasamy, father of Muthukumar - whose name on the passport was Rajendran - began to wail loudly. His wife, Pechiamma helped him to sit down.

"I swear I'll bury him also with my son.....mark it well, you old cow...." Rengasamy raved as he began rolling on the ground in grief and lamenting loudly. His wife and mother wept along with him.

"I'm absolutely sure he didn't hang himself....that fellow must have killed him and hung him up....why didn't you listen to me when I kept telling you not to send him abroad? Why have we been condemned to live to see our only son coming back as a corpse from a foreign land?" he moaned.

The three of them wept inconsolably.

Rengasamy tried to catch his breath while sobbing, and started hiccupping. He drank some water handed to him by his wife, and continued:

"The exact same thing happened to my grandfather....his own cousins poisoned him....my father always used to tell me that our enemies are not outsiders, they are our own family members....that has now been proved true once more.....I won't spare him....let him come out of the airport with my son's body, see if I don't chop him up..... if for any reason he doesn't turn up, I'll go to Arabia and kill him there itself...."

While weeping profusely, Rengasamy happened to glance at the shrine in the house. The idol of a female deity smeared in sacred ash seemed to be looking back at him. Every time he saw that idol, he would be reminded of carved pillars in temples and the statues adorning them. Looking at it, he would occasionally be reminded of the lion-headed sculptures in temples that had scared him during his childhood, and still caused a tiny frisson in his brain. The figure had been described to him as a mythological guardian creature known as the *yali,* by someone. Every time he looked at the figurine of the goddess, he would be reminded of the various animals making up the *yali* - lion, elephant, snake - and though he felt a twinge of fear and wished he could get rid of it, he could not bring himself to do so. Either because he felt it would be a sacrilegious act or else he did not want to go against his father's action, he simply let the statue remain in his home shrine.

That ancient statue, the figure of a woman wielding a sword, had been found some twenty years back when Rengasamy's father was digging a well in his field. He had secreted it in the folds of his *dhoti* and brought it home, installed it in the home shrine and began to worship it. On auspicious occasions, such as full moon and new moon days, he would conduct special ceremonies in its honour. Rengasamy had continued to follow his father's practice.

Rengasamy's mother, who observed him gazing at the idol, said, "Rengasamy, get rid of that idol.....ever since your father brought it home, it has brought nothing but bad luck to the house.... We've had to dispose of the land at Nayakkanur that your father had bought.... he also had to dispose of the four acres of land at Devankottai that your grandmother had received as dowry....it is said that it was all your grandmother's doing...." In the guise of blaming the idol, she was not too subtly running down her own mother-in-law and her daughter-in-law.

At this, Rengasamy's wife, Pechiamma, feeling insulted, leapt up and demanded, "What wrong have I done to this family that you speak like this? I demand to know what harm I'm supposed to have brought upon this family.....listen, you.....I'm not letting this matter go today.....come on, speak up.... ask your mother what catastrophe I've brought down upon this household....."

"Where do I start? You're the one who poisoned my grandson's mind and sent him abroad.... even when my son protested we didn't have the money to pay the agents their fees, didn't you collect the money from your brothers and arrange to send him overseas? Do you think we don't know about your trickery, you she-devil? You're the one responsible for my grandson's death, you hussy...." Rengasamy's mother wouldn't back down.

"Will I send my own son to die abroad, you old bat? Mind your words ...."

"They think we insulted their family and have done this purposely to destroy our family, Rengasamy....."

"Hold on....you're obviously dragging my family into this issue just to hide the fact that your own elder son's boy has killed my child..... old woman, you've only grown more bitter with age...."

"It was you who sent my grandson abroad to die....."

"Shut up, you witch....I'm not like you who cares more about herself than her own dead son...."

"Rengasamy, she's calling your mother a witch and you're keeping quiet?"

As their argument reached a peak and the two of them nearly came to blows, Rengasamy separated them and yelled at his mother to get out of the house.

His mother, Tulasiamma, went out in tears, stood in front of the house, strewed dust from the street at the house while continuing to harangue Pechiamma and Rengasamy. She then slowly went on her way.

As soon as she disappeared from view, Rengasamy turned to Pechiamma, gave her a resounding slap and yelled out, "You killed my son....." Not having expected this, she lost her footing, stumbled and fell down in a heap. While she had had her fair share of arguments with her husband, she had never once raised her hand against Rengasamy. Living in a village where even glaring at husbands was frowned upon, Pechiamma had forsaken all such conventions. She had the capability of trouncing her husband in an argument but had never considered raising her hand against him. Not because it went against the town's conventions, but because it might hurt her husband's fragile sensibilities. She got up and looking at Rengasamy, asked, "What are you saying?"

Rengasamy glared at her and, guessing what her response would be, thinking a step ahead said, "You encouraged him to go against me every step of the way, talk back to me disrespectfully and finally ended in offering him up as sacrifice. That innocent boy, who didn't know the ways of the world is now dead ...." Unable to continue, he began sobbing loudly.

Thinking in her mind that it was a surprise he had not raised this issue all these days, Pechiamma looked at Rengasamy and asked, "What do you mean I instigated him against you? It was you who sowed hatred in his mind against me, and you are now turning the table?"

"Shut up, you bitch....stop your theatrics....do you think I don't know how you kept filling his ears every time when I wasn't home? Who was responsible for sending him abroad over my objections? Wasn't it you who set him up against me just to take your own out on me? Bloody whore....why did you have to sacrifice my son for your own personal reasons?"

"Listen you, stop spouting nonsense like your mother, or you'll also end up suffering just like her, I tell you...."

"What suffering are you talking about? I've been hearing this for a very long time.....go on, call your brothers.....are you threatening me with them?"

"You're simply imagining things.....carry on like this and you'll end up becoming a raving lunatic sooner or later."

"Isn't that what you want?"

Pechiamma didn't reply. She simply got up and went into the kitchen.

She kept weeping and ranting to herself. Words such as 'police', 'jail', 'punishment' and 'orphan' were heard intermittently.

Rengasamy stood there listening to his wife's ravings while gazing fixedly at the idol of the goddess.

17

Shuja ibn Saqr al Zoubi al Sodari was seated in a Malayali *bufiya* (restaurant) at a village on the road to Najran. It was located some fifty kilometres from where Rajendran had dropped him off. The shops in the locality were just reopening after the Isha prayers.

He had ordered six pieces of *kubus hindi* (Indian bread), a plate of chilli chicken and a biriyani. When his order arrived, he first took a selfie with his phone camera and then started eating. Looking around the establishment, he started on the *hindi kubus* first. An Indian (Malayalam) news channel was telecasting an interview on the TV fixed to a wall in the restaurant. A correspondent was interviewing somebody on the show and it attracted Shuja's attention. He was in the habit of watching all the interviews on the TV regularly, especially those relating to history. He was determined to appear on a TV interview himself one day soon.

He took a mouthful of the biriyani while continuing to watch the TV. It was quite tasty and brought back memories of Afghanistan that were embedded deeply within his subconscious. There was also a strong reason why that memory, going back ten years in time, struck him now.

His *Walad Khal* (maternal cousin), Hassan ibn Ayidh al Sodari was returning home from England after obtaining his Master's degree there. Shuja, who had wished to organise a grand welcome for him,had been disappointed to find his relatives lukewarm to the idea when he mooted it to his group. He had been over the moon when Hassan announced his intention of going to the US to complete his doctorate in computer studies. More than science, Shuja had been attracted to the western philosophy that Hassan used to spout. Even though he did not understand half of what Hassan said, they made for interesting hearing. When Hassan had mentioned that his research involved a combination of science and philosophy, Shuja had been thrilled no end. He had gone around bragging to everyone that a kinsman from his *kabeela* was proceeding to America to carry out scientific research. But unfortunately Hassan had not been able to obtain a US visa.

Shuja grew livid at Hassan when he tried to explain that their family name 'al Sodari' was the cause for the denial of his visa. He questioned why the US Embassy had the al Sodari name on its watchlist. It appeared that a boy from another city, also named al Sodari, had gone to America for higher studies, got involved in terrorist activities and been imprisoned at Guantanamo. Shuja had to laugh at Hassan's explanation that this incident could have prompted the US to classify the entire al Sodari clan as a threat to their internal security.

It was one year after Hassan's departure for England that Shuja got a taste of that insidious poison. He learnt to his dismay that several men belonging to his indomitable al Sodari clan had been sucked into the vortex of Islamic terrorism being spawned in Afghanistan.

His cousin had also been caught up in its web and had gone off to Afghanistan. It was obvious that those who did not understand or appreciate the real implication of *jihad* were being misled and were proceeding down the wrong path. Hassan's parents had warned him that his chosen path was extremely dangerous apart from being against the tenets of Islam, but he had not heeded their words and had fled home to join a terrorist group. If they had reported the matter to the police, the entire family would come under suspicion and be treated as possible terrorists. If the other family members came to learn of it, they would pass snide remarks. They would gossip about it and snigger amongst themselves that the parents had failed to bring up their son properly. There was one more overreaching factor: the entire family would stand condemned in the eyes of their government which was engaged in a strenuous fight against terrorism. In view of this, Shuja's uncle decided that he needed to somehow quietly extract his son from the clutches of the terrorists. But he had no idea how to go about it.

Shuja's mother was deeply depressed at these goings-on. She decided there is just one person capable of performing this feat and that was her third son, Shuja. She turned to Shuja and ordered him, "I need you to bring back my brother's son. If you want to see me die in peace, I need to see my nephew in person again."

Shuja ibn Saqr al Zoubi al Sodari immediately took off after his cousin and spent a whole year searching for him in Afghanistan, Iraq and Syria. Those travels and their attendant problems flashed through his mind while eating biriyani at a *Hindi boofiya*. The trigger was the biriyani itself.

One day, while in Afghanistan, his hosts had prepared biriyani for him at their house on the hillside. It was the house of an Afghan working in Saudi as an upholsterer. His family had no connection whatsoever with any terrorist organisation. Wondering how he would make contact with the group, Shuja had just finished his biriyani and was relaxing in his room when loud voices were heard outside. He stood near the door trying to catch what was being said. But he did not understand the Afghani language. It was clear however that some outsiders had landed up there. They were not from an extremist group either...so, who were they? He listened closely to what was being said. Something told him he was in grave danger. He could hear the newcomers repeating "Saudi...Saudi," several times in an angry tone of voice, and concluded it was not going to end well for him. He reckoned that some Afghan working in Saudi had been mistreated by his Saudi employer, and the crowd that had gathered was eager to take it out on him. Memories of him quietly climbing up to the roof, removing some tiles to make an opening, jumping out and taking off for the capital, Kabul in the dead of the night, flashed before his eyes.

He also recalled how he had rescued his *Walad Khal* from an extremist group in Iraq and brought him back home. He felt proud of himself at his accomplishment. Every time he thought back of how he had cheated death, he felt a sense of accomplishment. He began to relish the biriyani along with the memory of how he had foxed the terrorist group and got away with his *Walad Khal* from under their very noses.

But some fresh questions were cropping up in his mind. Why was there hostility between nations like animosity that existed between humans? It was after all man who created artificial boundaries and established separate countries. While it was humans who operated these entities, it was but natural for their qualities to rub off on the country as a whole. But this does not hold good for the desert - no one can bring the desert's flow into any form of control. Whether it is Iran, Iraq, Saudia, America or Britannia - none of them can harness nature. Why did man create race, religion, nationality and similar concepts? Is it because some form of system was needed to control man's basic violent instincts? But, are not the same systems only aiding in fueling these vengeful feelings further?

How long will our hostility with the Al Mulaqim group continue?

Which generation will see it come to an end? Ya, allah! Will the absence of any form of controls or systems help bring it to a close?

Are the wars between countries similar to the feuds that fester between bedouin clans?

Can we ever live in peace with the Al Mulaqims?

Why not?

Some five years ago, when there was a dispute in the Aseer province between a *faqat* belonging to the Al Bethani *kabeela* and the Al Sheqrani *faqat* of our Al Sodari *kabeela* over water sharing, didn't all the Al Sodari clans put up a united front? We set all our differences aside then. If any bedouin group picks a fight with one of our *faqats*, all of us immediately unite against them.

It was not just a dispute between the Al Bethani *kabeela* and our Al Sheqrani *faqat*. It was a war between the Al Bethanis and the al Sodaris. On that occasion, we all stood together and defeated the Al Bethani *kabeela* and made them turn tail. That occasion saw us joining forces with our life-long enemy, the al Mulaqims to confront a common enemy. If we allied with them then, why can't we do it now?

There is evidence to establish that, when the land was in the grip of a famine two hundred years ago, we reached out to one another to survive the calamity. Those days were totally different from the present… it was the dark ages with no electricity. It is said that thousands perished in the desert with no food or water. Our elders then did not differentiate between various tribes or clans and ensured the survival of the remaining population by means of mutual cooperation.

Should only tough times bring people together? Why can't they get along with each other during normal times as well?

Why shouldn't we abandon the generations-old feud for the sake of our posterity? Some groups are waiting to take advantage of our hostility and manipulate it for their benefit. Extremist organisations appear as an attractive alternative to our youngsters. Our descendants deserve a better life. If we are serious about it, we need to give up our enmity with the al Mulaqims.

No, let them first renounce violence; we shall then follow suit.

They have killed my father's own brother. Only after I have settled that account, can there be peace and reconciliation. I need to prove myself to my family members, who presently talk slightingly of me, by committing an act that they have never committed before. I have proven myself several times earlier, but I have never committed a murder before. There's no other option. I'll do it.... I must do it. What if something happens to me as a consequence? Who is man enough to stand by me then? My *faqat* will protect me. I need to do this in order to preserve my *faqat*'s honour.

Shuja was secretly proud that he had accomplished several things that many considered as being beyond him. He was firmly of the opinion that, despite every obstacle, he could achieve anything he set out to do. It so happened that once an *asmar* (dark-skinned) Arab, named Mubarak bin Mohammed, had come seeking his help. Mubarak's family had once been slaves belonging to Shuja's household, and Mubarak himself was the great-great-grandson of the slave Bilal, who had been murdered by a Mulaqim. He was currently employed by a bank, slavery having been abolished by the government several years ago.

It was usual for former slave families to seek the help of their erstwhile owners in case of any problems. Following this practice, Mubarak had sought help from the family of Shuja bin Saqr al Sodari, who had been his ancestors' masters for ages. The family, who strictly followed the bedouin principle that it was their bounden duty to help those who approached them for assistance, nominated Shuja to stand by Mubarak and sort out his problem.

Mubarak's nephew, Misfir ibn Khalid, was a dentist in Riyadh. He had gone to Egypt and married a white girl. His life, which had been proceeding happily, had suddenly hit a snag after just two years of marriage.

A white Arab had visited Egypt and married Misfir's sister-in-law. When he had come to learn that his wife's elder sister was married to an *asmar*, he had gone to Riyadh, met with Misfir and picked an argument with him. He wanted Misfir to divorce his wife. Not knowing what to do or where to turn, Misfir had approached his uncle, Mubarak bin Mohammed seeking a solution. When he enquired who was advocating the divorce, Mubarak discovered that it was a rich *hadari* Arab. Unwilling to confront him directly, Mubarak had come to his erstwhile masters for a solution.

No one wished to get involved in this issue directly. But Shuja took the lead in the matter. Paying no heed to advice from others, he took the stand that it was his generation's duty to stand by the family of Bilal, whose great-grandmother had suckled his great-great-grandfather at birth, and proceeded directly to that rich *hadari* Arab's residence.

He had argued with the man loud and long, asserted his duty to safeguard the rights of his former slaves, fought hard in their defence and ultimately got the *hadari* himself to divorce his wife. But the outcome was not Shuja's doing alone. The *hadari*'s grandfather had also joined in the fray. Over a hundred years ago the al Zoubi bedouins had acted as protectors to that *hadari* family when they had been itinerant traders. Among those who plied their trade in *Hind*, Africa and Europe, these *hadaris* had also carried on their business, but had been targeted by several bedouin groups who used to plunder their wares. At such times, it had been Shuja's al Zoubi *faqat* members who had provided them with the necessary security. Five generations ago, when a renegade bedouin group had attacked their dwellings and made off with all their possessions, it had been Shuja's kinsmen who had caught the depredators and recovered most of their belongings. Keeping these facts in mind, the old *hadari* had ordered his grandson to divorce his wife. Unaware of these facts, Shuja continued to believe that he was the sole reason for the satisfactory outcome of the issue.

There have been many such incidents where he had patted himself on the back for a job well done. His ego received a further boost when there were comments that only he was capable of executing such daring feats. That is why once, when he became interested in acquiring a machine gun, he made contact with an underground group and clandestinely secured five of them. But before everyone could finish admiring his enterprise, the police came knocking at his door. Owning deadly assault weapons, other than a handgun for personal protection, was a serious offence and attracted a jail term in addition to a hefty fine.

To evade them, Shuja ibn Saqr ibn Ahmed al Zoubi al Sodari fled to the desert. He wandered around for six months and then surrendered to the police.

It had become a regular habit for him to commit some outrageous act or the other and run off into the unfettered freedom offered by the desert to escape the consequences. At those times, he would compose countless poems. While residing in the town, the memory of the desert would haunt him and while in the desert, passing sand dunes and hiding or roaming among stony mountains, he would feel the strong pull of the urban landscape. This conflicted state of mind affected him greatly. He often used to wonder whether this contradiction was common among all human beings. Is the human mind meant to be in a state of constant discord? Or, are the two aspects merely an eyewash and there is no real dichotomy? Is that why the human mind always works inconsistently? Does his unbounded inner mind refuse to accept the materialistic outer world created by human greed? Is that the root cause for this conflict? Could there be two minds inside one human body? Is inconsistency the basic foundation of a man's mind?

Musing over these questions, Shuja ibn Saqr al Zoubi al Sodari raised his head.

Most of the customers at the *boofiya* were from the subcontinent - Indians, Pakistanis and Bangladeshis. Its proprietor, a Malayali, was also quite familiar with his regular Arab patrons. He did not recognise Shuja, whom he thought was an outstation Saudi. At that moment, an elderly Arab walked in. He was an occasional client. Living in the *barr* (desert), he was in the habit of dropping in from time to time and purchasing fifty riyals' worth of parottas to go.

"As-salam alaykum," he greeted as he walked into the restaurant and took a seat.

"*Khamseen* (Fifty)?" the *bufiya* owner, Faisal from Malappuram in "God's Own Country" (Kerala), enquired of the elderly man.

The man responded grandly, "*Naam* (Yes)," to the query. He then noticed the back of another Arab at the next table and grew somewhat apprehensive.

He tried to slowly get up from his seat. But, when his chair made a scraping noise as he pushed it back, he grew irritated and sat down again.

Abandoning his biriyani, Shuja ibn Saqr al Zoubi al Sodari paid for his meal at the counter and turned back. He was now wearing his *ghutra* (head scarf) like a *luthma* (mask) over his face, with only his eyes visible. His hands were twitching. His heart was beating loudly enough to be audible. Unrecognisable in his mask, he gritted his teeth, took two steps forward and stood in front of the elderly Arab. He whipped out a pistol from the folds of his *thobe* with trembling fingers, steadied himself and shot the man thrice in the chest. He then took a picture of the man's dead body on his phone camera, ran out of the restaurant and jumped into a waiting Landcuiser and fled the spot.

Everyone at the *bufiya* sat there stunned. People came running from neighbouring shops. Some called the police and waited, shivering in fright. Meanwhile Shuja was racing like the wind. The elderly Arab's body lay where it fell on its back. His name was Khalid bin Abdullah bin Saad bin Turki bin Khalid bin Mohammed bin Abdullah al Mulaqim al Sodari.

And he belonged to the al Mulaqim *faqat* of the al Sodari *kabeela.*

18

Rengasamy was walking along the fields, with the idol of the goddess tucked in his *dhoti*. Having come to the conclusion that this ill-fated talisman was the cause of every blighted incident that had taken place in his household, he had decided to consign it back in the well where it had come from.

Memories of his son flashed into his mind suddenly and caused his heart to clench. Scenes of him playing about happily pricked his eyes and caused them to water. He squatted down in the field and, hitting himself on his head repeatedly with the statue, began to weep.

He had never made any demands. Even when his friends had teased him for coming to school barefoot, he had continued to attend classes without insisting upon proper footwear. He used to clean my bicycle every day when he was a young boy. At night, he used to lie outside the house, look up at the airplanes flying above and assert that he would be flying in them one day. In keeping with that dream, he had gone abroad in a plane and was now returning in another in a coffin.... It was all fated....

Rengasamy wept loudly as though his heart would break.

The pain which reached the pit of his stomach, settled there and provided him with some respite.

With his head bowed, several noises were rattling around in his skull. The words his wife had spoken before he left home were rebounding within his brain. She had spoken many words ... .peace, compromise, jail, police, conviction, orphan…and so on.

Thinking back, he let his gaze wander on the oxen tethered there. Could there be enmity in the animal kingdom too, he wondered.

His son had disappeared from his eyes. The huffing of the oxen induced fresh emotions and thoughts within him.

He looked all around him. The fields spread as far as the eye could see. Trees dotted the landscape. The sight of the horizon seemed to provide some relief to his fevered mind.

He took the bridles off the oxen and watched them take off in a run. He then turned to drop the idol into the borewell. He took three steps forward and stopped short, suddenly stunned.

A man was climbing out of the well!

It was a two thousand feet deep dry well. How could a man emerge from it?

A flustered Rengasamy rushed forward and asked him, “Hey, who're you? How did you get into this well?”

The man kept going on his way without responding.

Rengasamy again shouted, “Who're you?”

“I'm Mehboob Khan from Bihar. Rajendran told me my wife had come here for employment, and I'm looking for her,” he replied as he kept walking away.

A shocked Rengasamy yelled out, “Rajendran? Which Rajendran? Do you mean my son, Muthukumaran? Rajendran is the name on his passport....he was only sixteen when the passport was issued. So the agent got him a passport in someone else’s name. Didn’t he mention this to you? You are referring to my son, right? Isn’t he dead yet? Hey, you Bihari! Wait, tell me....stop, will you.....?”

The man silently walked a few more steps, then suddenly stopped, turned around and said, “Rajendran, the Madrassi....he works in the same town as me....he’ll come here tomorrow ... .you can see him then.....so, he’s your son, is he?” He then kept going without looking back.

A clueless Rengasamy watched his disappearing back for a few minutes, then turned and went towards the borewell again.

The entire place had turned aromatic. Some fragrant roots and sarsaparilla vines had suddenly sprouted inside the well.

Rengasamy bent down and peered into the darkness of the well. He then turned once again to look in the direction where the Bihari had gone. He was nowhere to be seen! When he turned towards the left for a better look, he was met with a startling sight. A horse was seen moving around there with its muzzle sniffing the ground as though it was trying to catch a scent. Whose horse is this? Is it the Bihari’s? Where did it come from?

Who was the Rajendran the Bihari mentioned?

He said they were both employed in the same town. Was he referring to my son? That means he’s also from Arabia. If so, when did he come here?

Could it be that he came via an underground route? But, is there such a route? If I took that road, would I be able to reach my son?

Someone seemed to approach him. Rengasamy turned abruptly.

The horse was licking the idol of the sword-wielding goddess with its tongue.

Rengasamy stood there stunned at the sight.

Is this a horse from around here? Or, like that Bihari, is it an Arabian horse that had come up from the well?

A thousand questions bombarded Rengasamy's brain and caused him to shiver.

Could this be an idol of my grandmother's family deity, Pechiamman? Is the guardian deity of this village, Karuppusamy seated on the horse, invisible to my eyes? Oh, Rajendran was just five years old that day when the sugarcane crop I had planted in this very field caught fire. No, not caught fire….it was deliberately set on fire….was it really my father who was behind that act? All these days I have been blaming my elder brother for it and waiting for an opportunity to take revenge on him by killing off his cows … .But it is clear to me now…..Sundar - my nephew and my son's killer - had done it at my father's instigation. I now get the message behind the eye signals the two of them exchanged that day.

He burst out crying once again. He wished he could die. But, at the next moment, he dried his eyes, took a long breath and told himself:

"Renga, no, don't die now….Sundar's certain to come home next year … .kill him as soon as he lands here … .you shouldn't die now….. yes, that's right….I won't die until I've killed the man who murdered my son….it doesn't matter that my father, who told him to set fire to my sugarcane field, is dead and gone…..I'll go after him and kill him too……I won't die now…."

He bent down and peered into the well.

The sky was reflected there.

The sweet aroma of the sarsaparilla vines blended with the breeze and swirled around the horse and the idol of the goddess, causing both to rise up in the air.

As the breeze suddenly transformed into the sound of the *udukkai* (hourglass drum), Rengasamy stood stunned when he beheld the flying horse.

Is it a horse? Or a lion? Or was it an elephant? Or else, was it a combination of all three? How is it able to soar in the air with no wings? It's paddling the air with its lion's paws…. It has a trunk and tusks like an elephant….And, who's that seated on its back? Is it my son, Muthukumaran? Has he come just like that Bihari told me? That means he's not dead! Did he fly here all the way from Arabia on the back of this beast? No….this is not my son….my son is a young man…..then, who's this? Is it Karuppusamy? Oh, I smell the fragrance of sandalwood in the air….

Oh! What's happening? He's slashing his own throat….stop…..sir, please don't….don't…. Hahaha…..you're the priest, aren't you? And you're worshipping yourself? What? It is a joke? What did you say? You're going to destroy my entire bloodline by means of this ritual? Hey, who're you? Get down, you old man…..come and get me, if you can…..you bastard…. Come on….

Saying this, Rengasamy leapt forward to seize the horse and its rider.

19

It has been two weeks since Shuja ibn Saqr al Zoubi al Sodari had taken refuge in the desert amidst the mountains. Having shot dead an elderly man belonging to a rival *faqat* at a Malayali *bufiya* in Damra, he had escaped into the desert and, after changing his hideout four times, had reached his current location. He had also made it clear to his brother-in-law, who came to meet him in secret once, not to come back again, and that he was quite capable of looking after himself. He had however requested that his family take special care of his daughter, Rabiya. He also made arrangements for someone or the other to drop in on him from time to time and provide him assistance in the midst of that limitless desert, where he was currently surviving without a telephone or means of transport. In these days of the internet, there were a thousand and one ways of ensuring a helping hand. One such aid was the satellite telephone.

He had secreted a satellite phone at a spot some five kilometres away from his actual hideout. At the second half of every third night he would dig it up and make a call to one of his trusted family members and disclose his actual location. He would then make arrangements for the necessary supplies to be delivered by friendly bedouin groups nearby, and then quickly move to another hiding spot. At areas where this support was not available, he would sustain himself by catching a *dabb* or a bird and, on occasions, even a stray camel calf, to relieve his hunger. But he had been unable to get a proper night's sleep. He suffered from the shakes in the middle of the night, and the face of the man he had killed would suddenly appear in front of his eyes and cause him tremors.

He needed to endure this exile until, unable to get at him and exact their revenge, his enemies killed one of his brothers and settled their score. In addition, the police would also be on the look-out for him. He therefore needed to continue this nomadic existence for several more months. His enemies however would not seek police assistance. They would not rest until they themselves had exacted retribution from him for killing a man belonging to their *faqat*. If the police also took an active interest in investigating the matter, fugitives such as him might have to stay underground for the rest of their lives. Alternatively, they could flee to a neighbouring country.

This is how the person he had shot, Khalid ibn Abdullah al Mulaqim al Sodari, had fled to Iraq several years ago after killing an al Zoubi clan member. Having been unable to catch hold of him, despite their long and strenuous search, the al Zoubis had finally extracted their retribution by killing his brother. When news of this reached him, Khalid had ended his decades-long exile and returned home to Arabia. He was no longer worried about being in the al Zoubis' cross-hairs, since the blood debt had been paid. The men of the al Zoubi *faqat* also did not attach any importance to his return, since they considered the score settled. But Shuja was not one to let go. Having learnt that the wanted man was now living in Tamra, he had caught a lift from Rajendran, gone into the town and shot Khalid dead at the Malayali restaurant.

Like Shuja, Khalid bin Abdullah bin Saad al Mulaqim al Sodari, who had been shot dead at the Indian eatery, had killed a man belonging to the al Zoubi *faqat* several years ago and vanished into the vast reaches of the desert. After remaining hidden for several years in the desert, he had decided to sneak into Iraq reasoning that none of his enemies would venture so far in search of him. But, before moving to Iraq, he had allied himself for some time with a desert group involved in robbing caravan trains. Then, tiring of holding up travellers and divesting them of their belongings, he switched sides and joined hands with another bedouin group that provided protection to trading caravans. Finally, fed up with this lifestyle, he left the area and proceeded north towards Iraq. He contemplated hiding out in the ancient city of Baghdad and turned his horse in that direction. He even thought of advancing his education in that centre of ancient learning. However he ended his journey half-way there, instead of actually landing up in Baghdad.

That was the time when both the world wars had ended and a new country called Iraq had come into being. He began living with a bedouin group located in the deserts of Iraq.

That was also the time when the westerners discovered oil under the desert's sands. The government, in collaboration with foreign oil companies, was turning the desert into a vast oilfield. It was consolidating the various territories that were under different bedouin *kabeelas* within the new states' boundaries. Some of the *kabeelas* refused to part with the land that had been in their possession over many generations. The government was holding talks with such groups and, with the help of the other supportive groups, concluding understandings with them. The bedouin groups, that had existed for ages on the basis that each *kabeela* had its own territorial limit, did not easily comprehend terms such as 'development' and 'one nation'. They proclaimed 'this is our land and no one has the right to it but us'. The government was struggling to convince them that times were changing.

Khalid ibn Abdullah al Mulaqim al Sodari, from Najd in Arabia, was living with one such bedouin group. As per their sheikh's directive, no one in the group was in favour of surrendering his land to the oil companies. Even as the various *kabeelas* opposed to the government's proposal were planning to ally themselves to fight against the state, Khalid became a bridge between the two sides and sorted out the issue amicably. It was agreed that a share of the revenue from the oil production would go to the Bedouins and their children would be provided with prominent positions in the government. On the basis of this understanding, the oil companies had begun their work in the desert.

Having sorted out this issue somehow, but worried that word of it might get back to Arabia, Khalid ibn Abdullah al Mulaqim al Sodari once again dived into the trackless desert. He kept moving from place to place in the company of nomadic bedouin groups for several more years. He then somehow convinced them that they needed to put an end to their itinerant lifestyle and provide their descendants with a stable life, and took up their cause with the Iraqi government. However, the negotiations did not pan out as expected and he then began talks with the government of Kuwait. But those talks too ended in failure. The nomads had no documents to prove they belonged to either country. When the new Arab nations were formed, the bedouins, unwilling to confine themselves within their boundaries, had preferred the trackless expanse of the desert and its towering dunes. Ignoring the government's directive that they should register their names and dates of birth with the government, they continued their life as nomads in the desert. After oil was discovered in their lands, the state tried to corral them all within its territory. But unwilling to be controlled by any regulatory authority, these bedouins preferred to spread out in the desert rather than confine themselves within a single country's boundaries. While they lived their days fearlessly in the blistering heat and numbing cold of the desert, they did sometimes feel like providing their children with a stable, settled life. But they possessed no valid documentation to prove they belonged to any particular country. That is why all the efforts of Khalid bin Abdullah had ended in failure. Asking them to try their luck in Arabia, he made his way back to Iraq. When he arrived there, the Iraq-Kuwait war had just ended. He cursed himself for having wasted his time in the desert, completely unaware of the unfolding events. He rued the fact that he had played no part in the war. After a few years, when the Islamic State came into being, he enrolled several bedouin groups who lacked any identity papers into the movement and even fought along with them for a while. When the conflict intensified, he escaped and scattered along with the bedouin groups back into the desert. He had then come to learn that his brother had been killed in retaliation for the murder he had committed. Laughing out loud at this development, he dubbed his enemies 'worthless twats' and travelled back to Arabia clandestinely, in a black GMC van provided to him by the SISI, ending several decades of exile, and had settled down in his native town. Having come to know of this, Shuja, belonging to the al Zoubi *faqat*, had gone to Tamra and gunned him down at the Malayali *bufiya*. He then uploaded a photo of the dead Khalid al Mulaqim on his WhatsApp post to three of his *faqat* members with a note reading, "You need to kill the real murderer, you wimps ... .not his brother". He had then smashed his telephone to pieces and escaped into the desert.

Following two weeks of running after killing the elderly man, Shuja had arrived at this location. Running and changing hiding spots constantly, he had now found refuge in a place surrounded by hills and rocks. The original panic having passed, his eyes reflected a sense of internal peace.

It was a stretch of desert that consisted of some fifty kilometres of mountain ranges and contained some of the most fertile soil in the region. While the Rub' al Khali or the empty quarter, the blistering hot part of the Arabian desert, was all sand and massive dunes located in the southern part, this mountainous area of the desert was situated in the north and consisted of arable land. As you proceed eastwards, tall mountains covered with a profusion of trees and plants mark the end of the desert, and the area witnesses regular rainfall and contains cultivable land. The northeast is where the oil is. But that area is also a hive of police activity. It is impossible to hide out in the Rub' al Khali as not a drop of water is available there. Moreover, that area does not fall within the al Zoubi jurisdiction. East is al Mulaqim territory. The north alone is safe. As it contains territory that belongs to the al Zoubi *faqat*, it is very secure. Having decided that if he wandered around in the northern part of the desert, without venturing into any town, he would be safe from both the police as well as the al Mulaqims, Shuja ibn Saqr al Zoubi al Sodari was hiding in a cave in a hill with all his senses on high alert. As it had been two weeks since he arrived at the spot, he was planning to move out of the hideout that night.

From his hiding place he noticed that three bedouin youngsters, who were making their way across the desert, seeking a suitable location before summer set in, had camped close to his cave along with their *ibals* (camels). He had heard the sound of human voices three days ago and, lying prone on the top of the cave, had noted their arrival. They were slowly making their way across the desert, at the rate of two kilometres a day, with their camels. They had a Landcruiser jeep with them and carried walkie-talkies, telephones and laptops. They looked like school students. At nights, they made their way to a caravan parked some ten kilometres away to spend the night in it. The caravan was equipped with air conditioners and had toilet and kitchen facilities. Shuja had watched them carefully for two days. He was not sure if they had come here, along with their Ethiopian retainers, to graze their camels in compliance with their parents' directives, or to avoid attending school/college.

Once he satisfied himself that they had no visitors dropping in on them, Shuja considered approaching them for help. He also first thought of creeping closer to listen to them speak to ascertain what *kabeela* they belonged to. He also wondered if he should wait for them to retire to the caravan for the night and make enquiries of their Ethiopian servants instead. But he finally concluded that any such move would only end up endangering him, and waited for them to move closer to his hiding place. They were most certainly al Sodaris. No other bedouin group would frequent this area because it fell within the al Sodari territory. Shuja happened to have crossed the al Zoubi *faqat*'s area and was now in territory belonging to another *faqat*. He had also decided in his own mind how he should identify himself in case the youngsters stumbled upon him.

There were still two nights left before the men from this area were scheduled to visit him and help him relocate. Somehow, this time when he spoke to them, their tone of voice had carried a different timbre. Were the police planning to trap him through them? Let me wait and see ... I'll talk to them once more on the satellite phone after these youngsters have left the area. I'll then lie in wait on the top of the cave and watch their arrival. I'll not reveal my exact location to them. He decided he would track them to see if any outsiders came along with them or anyone followed them to the meeting spot..

The young bedus finally neared his hiding spot. He took cover within the cave and carefully monitored their conversation. Most of their talk revolved around football and the latest model of cars. He still kept his gun cocked and ready. As the Ethipians slept at the edge of the rock, he tiptoed past them silently and went to where their camels were tethered. He rummaged through the bag on the back of one of them and removed some snacks, a bottle of water and a plastic net hidden in a secret compartment, and quietly sneaked back into his cave.

The next morning, after they had gone some distance from where he was hiding, he came out of the cave, inhaled the desert air with relief, locked his hands above his head and stretched comfortably. The sun's rays felt good on his body.

Their presence still seemed to linger in the area. That was when an image of Ali appeared before his eyes and caused him to burst out laughing. Ali was a *hadari* Arab who had studied with him in school. He was a handsome boy with a soft voice. Ali's father had enrolled him in a bedouin school, instead of at a school in the *hadari* area, hoping that his son would grow up to be as fearless as the bedouins through regular contact with them. But, from *mutha vassal* (primary school) through to *tanuviya* (secondary school), there was no change in him. In those schools, meant exclusively for boys, he was the only one with a feminine face and tone of voice. As a result he faced a constant threat of being abducted. There were just three or four boys that Ali could truly call friends, and Shuja was one of them. Once, while some persons had tried to kidnap Ali, Shuja had fought them off and saved him. They had both been fifteen at that time. For some reason, Shuja recollected the times Ali and he had studied together, played together and spent time together at mountainous places like this one,and the thought had provoked his sudden burst of laughter. But the laughter soon induced a twinge of sadness within him.

After *mutha vassal* and throughout *tanuviya* and *jamiya* (university), he recalled the pain of his teachers' and classmates' taunts, laughter and snide comments. Whenever they saw bedouin students trying to get the hang of smartphones or access the internet, they would laugh out loud and pass comments such as, "*Huva Bedu* (Bloody Bedouin), *mush aaraf* (it's beyond them)". He would get very angry at such times. But, tamping down that feeling, he would mentally vow, "Yes, I'm a bedu.....but one day, you'll come begging to me asking me to teach you stuff ... .I'll show you then what a bedu is capable of ...." But one aspect caused him immeasurable pain. He constantly wondered whether the new technological era was leaving bedus like him behind. He also remembered how big cities such as Riyadh had left him awestricken. He had felt sad that several of his clansmen had been unable to take advantage of any of the government's welfare schemes due to their backwardness and lack of awareness. When visiting other Arab countries too, he had often faced discrimination because of his bedouin background.

For the past four or five years Ali and he had been regularly taking vacations abroad during their holidays. As there were no real touristy spots to visit in Arabia, he and others like him had been going abroad on their vacations.

He now recalled some of his trips. The sorrow that the killing had robbed him of future such jaunts overwhelmed him suddenly. He shook himself free of such thoughts and surveyed the landscape around him with a sigh.

He scrutinised the spot vacated by the young men closely. Cursing them mentally for having sparked off old memories, he carefully scanned the area. He looked for anything useful they might have left behind. Nothing was to be found. Camel droppings brought thoughts of *kabsa* to his mind, and his mouth watered. He wished he could have at least snatched one of their camel calves. Immediately, another thought struck him and he rushed into his cave.

He retrieved the plastic net, draped it round his neck and went around the hill to check if any dead birds could be found. There were none around, though a few feathers could be seen scattered around. In a few minutes, as he had hoped, two crows came and perched on the rock. He lay still, collected a stone and began watching the crows' movements. Both of them flew down and began pecking at the pieces of *kubus* left behind by the young men and their servants. Watching their movements keenly, Shuja threw a stone as hard as he could at them as they were busy squabbling over the food scraps. The stone thrown with a lot of force hit one of the birds' wings and thudded hard against the other's chest. As the injured bird lay flapping on the ground, unable to fly, the other crow began to wheel overhead, cawing loudly. Holding his robe with one hand, Shuja darted forward and quickly picked up the injured bird with one hand. He lobbed another stone hard at the other crow flying above. It attempted to flap its wings and fly higher, but its injured wing, unable to bear its weight, brought it crashing down to the ground. Shuja collected the second bird also, tied them both to the end of the plastic net and went around to the other side of the rock.

This was the spot where he had observed desert falcons, known as *sagers*, arriving from time to time, over the past five days. Three days ago, he had attempted to bring one of them down by throwing stones at a flock of them. But the *sagers*, a hundred times faster than him, had escaped into the sky before the stones had even reached anywhere near them. His plan was to snare one of them and train it to catch birds flying at a far distance, and bring them back to him. But, as though they could read his mind, the *sagers* kept their distance from him. He had then rued the fact that he did not possess a net with which to trap the tricky raptors. He had searched high and low for a net of some sort but had not been able to lay his hands on one. That is why he had stolen the net belonging to the Ethiopian servants of the bedouin youngsters. His guess that they might have nets to trap *sagers* had proved right. As a well-trained *sager* could sell for thousands of riyals in the black market, the Ethiopians had secreted the net in a hidden compartment in a bag on one of the camels. That was the net he had stolen and was going to use to catch the desert's strongest bird and ruler of its skies.

He spread the net out and placed the crows on it. The *sagers* would spot the birds and swoop down to feed on them. He fashioned the net in such a way that it would envelop the falcons as soon as they landed on it. Anticipating the moment when the *sagers* would be trapped in the net as soon as they swooped down on the bait, he lay down at a distance and tried to breathe softly and noiselessly.

He lifted his head and scanned the sky. Not a bird was visible. As he was wondering whether the Ethiopians could have possibly captured all the *sagers* in the area, a formless question worried him. They were the words spoken by the Ethiopians in their half-asleep state. He delved into his brain to analyse those words. Their words now came back to him hard and impacted his brain.

Even though he did not know their language, the occasional use of the term 'bedu' and the scornful laughter that accompanied it now caused his brain to heat up. When he recalled that this word had been accompanied by the term *kelb* (dog), he wished he could rush after them and kill them all. He turned to look at the sand that spread out beneath the mountain. His heart calmed a bit at its sight.

The next moment, all thoughts about the Ethiopians vanished and the issue of *asmar* and *hadari* Arabs entered his mind. The Blacks, who had earlier been our slaves, now behaved like equals and occupied prominent government positions. Similarly, the *hadaris,* who were earlier our subordinates, are now dominating in all the sectors. Would we, the bedus, destroy ourselves with our internecine conflicts? This fear sparked another question in his mind: who were the original inhabitants of this land?

We have lived here for over a thousand years. We were here even before Islam was born. Aren't we the original settlers of this land? Some of the Blacks claim they were the earliest race in this region ... .hahaha.....they seem to have forgotten that my ancestors brought them here in chains from Africa as slaves.....

It is true that we bedouins came here from Yemen originally. But the Blacks' claim that we subsequently grabbed their land and subjugated them is a total lie. It is said that when my great-great-grandfather purchased some *asmars* at the Riyadh market and brought them home, his sister, after one look at their dark, terrifying forms, had dropped dead from fright! So, what does that prove? That we were the original inhabitants of Najd, right? Wasn't there a major argument on social media recently? An eccentric poet from Kharj belonging to the al Vadhamin *faqat* had uploaded a video on twitter of his song, claiming that his people were the original settlers from Yemen. Our people had given an appropriate response to that nonsensical claim. What had that foolish poet said in his song? That, prior to the introduction of Islam, it was their girl goddess that everyone worshipped! He claimed that there was historical evidence that, not just the Nabati rulers but even the Roman emperors used to fall at the feet of that girl and offer homage to her. He must have released that song simply to stir up controversy. Our folklore clearly states that people of his *faqat* were in fact the underlings and servitors of the Roman emperors. Just because some of our ancestors served as provincial governors to Farsi rulers and paid them tribute, how can it be claimed that we were slaves of the Iranians? Even if it were so, those events took place some two thousand years ago. During the pre-Islamic *jahiliyyah* period. It is not acceptable to call us flunkeys to the Iranians for that reason alone. Even though the *hukuma* (government) has banned use of such offensive language in poems and on social media, they continue to taunt us in this fashion. We should teach them a fitting lesson soon.

With the proliferation of platforms such as twitter and instagram, the poets who sing of olden times have received a new lease of life. Why can't they instead compose worthy poems like mine? But, no. They insist on singing about olden times and dividing the civil society….. bloody crackpots….

While thinking on these lines, another thread started running through Shuja's mind….

Perhaps, only two feelings - affection and antagonism - run through our bedu veins…..is there no end to it? Didn't our history commence with unbounded attachment and unbridled animosity? Poets of yore, such as Jarir and Al Aqthal , have violently disagreed with each other and sung about the first great epic battle..... I'm told that the saga is even today being aired as a serial on a Turkish TV channel.

These battles, that took place between the *kabeelas* of our aboriginal groups in Syria's mountainous regions, are still spoken of in this world, two and three thousand years later. The most famous of the bedouin *kabeela* battles during the pre-Islamic times was the forty-year one between the Taqlibs and the Baqrs. To wreak vengeance on Jassim of the Baqr *kabeela*, who had killed his elder brother, Sheir Salam had wiped out the entire Baqr *kabeela*. Being descendants of that proud Banu Taqlib lineage, should we be scared of those Banu Sayid men? We were the very first people to migrate from Syria to Yemen and then move to Najd. But, what do they claim? Having been evicted from Yemen by their own forefather, these descendants of Banu Sayid claim that they were the first people to come to Najd! Hahaha....we, the Taqlibi scions, have been here a thousand years before Islam made its appearance. For generations, we have been this land's true heirs. From being nomads, our race slowly became agriculturists and cultivators. It was only later that those Banu Sayids arrived at the scene. They probably appeared only after the advent of Islam. Ever since their arrival, there has been a state of constant conflict between us. If they tried to usurp our land, are we Taqlibis supposed to simply grin and bear it? We are, after all, the direct descendants of the Adnan *kabeela*..... we are the historic Taqlibi .... What? There was never anyone named Sodari? Are you saying that the Taqlibis and the Banu Sayid called a truce among themselves and allied under an imaginary progenitor named Sodari to fight another bedouin group in the east, called the Vasbehis? Who said so? Those cowards belonging to the Banu Sayid group might have concocted such an imaginary tale just to join forces with us. We are not such weaklings to create an imaginary character called Sodari and live under his shadow. Aren't we the Taqlibs who stood up bravely against the Kuveshis and the entire al Rehthans? Everything you post on Twitter and Instagram is not the gospel truth. We know how to combat such vile propaganda. We may have a thousand disagreements between the al Zoubis and the al Mulaqims, but lay a finger on our clan's honour and you'll feel the sharpness of our swords....

Shuja glanced at the net. No *sager* had been snared yet. He jumped off the rock, went into the cave, had a drink of water, collected some snacks and returned to his spot on the rock to keep an eye on the net.

The evening sun pricked his eyes and woke him up from his nap. He lifted his head and looked at the net. It was still bare. He jumped down, removed the crows from the net and threw them aside. As he began rolling up the net, he heard the screeching of falcons and looked up at the sky.

He climbed up the rock and looked again. Nothing was visible. He went into the cave, packed his possessions in a plastic bag and set out.

He looked all around him as he walked along cautiously. He proceeded to the spot where his satellite phone was hidden.

He had a brief conversation with the person who was supposed to come and help him relocate, quickly passed on information about the new spot he had picked out, and began heading towards it.

He walked with the aid of the stars, sat down for a moment where the sand dunes began, and took a short breather. He then began negotiating the mounds and increased his pace.

When he was certain he had reached the centre of the sandbars, he turned southwards. As he was climbing up and down the sand dunes in the wan light of the moon, he thought he heard human voices. He immediately lay down at the foot of a sandbank and warily watched the ridge in front of him. He could now clearly hear two persons conversing. A man and a woman. Their voices did not seem to be moving towards where he lay hidden, and he once again attuned his ears to their conversation. Yes, the sound was coming from a fixed location. He got up, climbed the sand dune and looked all around him. Where the sand dunes ended, towards the north, and fertile soil commenced, he saw their tent. He began slowly walking towards it.

He once again lay down on top of the dune nearest to the camp and cautiously surveyed the area. The tent seemed to belong to an elderly man and a girl. Before making a move towards them, he kept still, watching them for a while, and scanning the area around them. He then began to slowly move towards the camp. From a distance, he loudly greeted them saying, "As-salamu alaikum". The old man turned to face him calmly, as though he had been awaiting his arrival, and responded with a totally unflustered, "Harhab."

Shuja responded equally politely, "Al Bega", and made his way towards the man. It was only when he neared him did he realise that the old man was sightless. He kissed him on his forehead formally and shook his hand. Both exchanged the customary Arabic greetings, enquiring after each other's welfare, which is quite an elaborate ritual in itself.

"Kayf haluk?"

"Asak tayyib?"

"Hu shlonak?"

"Hushlon Ahleq?"

"Hushlon Rabbeq?"

"Hushlon Jamateq?"

"Hushlon min Ishsheleq?"

"As ssa ma qlaf?"

"Keefaq dhoudh?"

"Asak tayyib?"

"Kayf haluk?"

"Asak tayyib?"

"Arhab, arhab"

"Al bega, al bega"

After having exchanged some twenty or so such enquiries after each other's health and wellbeing, the old man sat Shuja down on a blanket and offered him dates and *kahwah* (black tea).

When the elder began the conversation with, "I expect it to rain very heavily next week. Make sure you're in a secure place before then, young man," Shuja masked his shock in the darkness of the night, and politely responded with, "I'll certainly do so, sir."

When, in turn, he asked which *kabeela* he belonged to, the old man replied, as though anticipating the question, 'al Mulaqim', and immediately smilingly reassured Shuja, "Don't worry, *valadh* (son), I have no connections with the Mulaqims belonging to your town." Who is he? Was he already aware that I have killed a man belonging to their *faqat*? Could he be the bait in a trap set for me? Flustered at these thoughts, he rose and said, "I'll take your leave now, sir. Thank you very much for your hospitality. May God guard you. Insha' allah, we shall meet again soon. *Ma Salama* (goodbye)." As he turned to leave, the old man grasped his arm and, employing the authoritative tone of bedouin elders, thundered, "Where do you think you're going? You can't leave my place without having eaten something first. *Tham, ya rajjal, tham... ijlis* (sit down)" Unable to resist, Shuja sank down while letting his eyes wander around to see if anyone else was lurking at the spot.

The old man arranged some logs in front of the tent, set them alight and suspended a whole sheep on a spit over the fire. Shuja wondered how, despite being unable to see, he performed all these acts so dexterously.

"What did you say your name was? Shuja ibn Saqr, right?"

"Yes sir."

"Hmmm...and your daughter is now three and half?"

His whole body seemed to be on fire. He stared at the man and asked, "How do you know about my daughter, *Thawweel Al Omer*?"

"Didn't you mention her a few minutes ago? You even told me her name. It's Rabiya, isn't it?" the old man laughed out loud and added, "you shouldn't forget things in your fright ... .it'll make you vulnerable and easier for your enemies to track you down. Always be on your guard, *ya valadh*.... Got it?"

Shuja immediately got up, snatched the gun concealed under his *thobe*, aimed it at the old man and loudly demanded, "Who're you? How come you're talking about things that I haven't even told you about? You Mulaqim dog, have you been sent here to trap me?"

The old man merely laughed out loud at this outburst. He suddenly bent down, grabbed a fistful of sand and flung it into Shuja's eyes.

Shuja slid down a sand dune, rolled and clawed furiously at his eyes to clear his vision as he straightened up.

There was a Landcruiser SUV in front of him. He wiped his eyes clean and opened them wider.

Scared at the sight of the jeep, he attempted to quickly climb up a sand dune.

He stopped when the man behind the wheel hailed him. He looked around cluelessly. There were sand dunes all around. This was the very last one. Below it began the stretch of fertile, agricultural land.

Oh! It is our contact - the man from our *faqat* whom I had asked to meet me at the appointed place. But how did I land here? Where is that old man? Did he escape after throwing sand in my eyes? No, that is impossible ... .could he have dismantled his tent, collected all his possessions and disappeared so fast? If so, was he an illusion or was he for real? Could that man have been the king of Nabati poetry, Al Dindan? No, that was impossible....Dindan's been dead for many years now. A European research scholar had met him and had published a selection of his bedouin poetry. While his poems have reached readers in Europe and America, most of our own people are still unaware of his work. There are several poets far greater than him in our *faqat* too. Could it be his son whom I encountered? But it is said Al Dindan was a bachelor. If so, who was that old man? How did he know so much about me and my life?

The man who had come to fetch Shuja asked, "It was a *jinn* ... .*you* must have encountered a *jinn*. It must have come to deliver a message to you ... .what did it say, my friend?"

At this, Shuja burst out laughing and said, "Forget *jinns* .... Let's go, pal." But the man did not let go that easily. "You know what it says in the holy book? There are both good *jinns* and bad *jinns* ...." he went on and cited several examples to back up his argument. Shuja merely listened without responding, simply making appropriate noises at the right intervals, while keeping a lookout to see if any other vehicle was following them.

Shuja was deposited among another range of mountains and the landcruiser sped on its way.

It was a very tall mountain. Shuja climbed up to its top and looked around at the landscape. The mountain was round in shape with a pool of water in the middle. He climbed down slowly. He decided it was a secure spot and planned to spend a few days there. He could see no signs of any human activity in the area and, reassured, he lay down to sleep.

As soon as the sun rose, he performed the *fajr* prayer and once again surveyed the location. There were several secure caves in which he could hide if the need arose. There was an adequate supply of good drinking water in the form of rainwater which had collected to form pools. He had with him enough food supplies to last him for two weeks. Thinking he would plan his next move after a fortnight, he scooped up some water from the pool and sniffed at it. There was no odour. He drank some of it and splashed some on his face and then inspected the pus-filled abscess festering on his right leg. As it looked about ripe to burst, he pinched it with his fingernails. It ruptured with a wet sound and oozed pus. He took some water in the palm of his right hand and cleaned it out. Took some sand and applied it to the spot.

As he got up, he felt as though someone was watching him, and a thrill ran through his body. He carefully glanced all around him. No one was visible. Worried that another person could also be hiding out at the spot, he yelled out, "*As salam alaikum.*" No response was forthcoming. He shouted out again, "*Min, ya rajjal? Tha'al barra* (Who's that? Come out)" and, producing his pistol, looked around cautiously.

There was no reply. Was it only my imagination or could it be a *jinn,* as that fellow suggested?

Auzu Billahi Minashaitanir Rajeem,

Bismillahir Rahamanir Rahim....

As he began eating his *kubus* Shuja began wondering, 'that Indian fellow, what is his name.... Rashendran..... Maybe I should have brought him along?'

A sudden fear gripped his mind.

He began to sing one of his compositions. He also began contemplating moving away from the current spot.

As he started reciting a second poem, a *sager* came whizzing by and perched by the pool. He looked at it in astonishment. After determining it was in no hurry to fly away, he carefully removed the net he had wound around his waist and, moving soundlessly by the rock, he went near the pool and swiftly cast the net over the bird. He timed his throw to coincide with the moment the bird dipped its beak into the pond to drink. He was well aware of the *sagers*' speed - especially the two-toned ones.

To his own surprise, the *sager* was trapped within the folds of the net. He simply couldn't believe his luck. He jumped up in elation, lifted the net with the bird, removed his *ghutrah* and swaddled the *sager* within its folds like a baby, and gently stroked its head. The bird put up a brief struggle and tried to peck at his hands initially, but soon calmed down.

Shuja knew all about caring for a captured falcon. It needed to be wrapped up in a piece of cloth and tended like a child for thirteen days. It needed to be hand-fed. He was also well aware of its dietary needs. But, currently, he had no special bird fare with him to offer. He therefore began feeding it with whatever he had on hand. Some bedus preferred the *shaheen* (peregrine falcon) over the *sager*. But Shuja personally fancied *sagers* over the *shaheens*, though the latter were much more desired and fetched hundreds of thousands of riyals in the market. His heart would melt every time he fondled a *sager*. He felt the same feeling overwhelm him this time around as well.

He took some water in his cupped palm and offered it to the bird. It slurped it up through its beak.

Within just two days, the bird began to follow a few simple instructions. He kissed it and made up a poem about it on the spot. It screeched in response as though singing a poem of its own. For some reason it reminded Shuja of the Taif *mohavara*. Like the pre-Islamic Okaz poetry competition, the *mohavara* was also a contest among poets. Poets from all over Arabia would flock to Taif with their poems and vie with one another to win the prizes on offer for the best compositions.

Till three years ago, Shuja was in the habit of visiting every single poetry competition within Arabia. His ultimate aim was to win the million dirham *sha'er al million* poetry competition in the Emirates once he had won at least one of the competitions in Arabia. But, so far he had never managed to win even one of the local competitions. He had however distinguished himself at several of the *mohavara* competitions. The *mohavara* is a talent contest between two poets. The second poet is expected to sing a composition in line with the verse recited by the first person. The first poet would kick off the competition with a two- or three-line rhyme teasing his opponent. The second poet would respond with a suitable rejoinder on the same lines. Some ten-fifteen men, standing in front of the poets, would echo their lines singing them out loud, while shaking their bodies in rhythm. If a proper riposte was not forthcoming, or a poet could not come up with an appropriate verse in response, that poet would be deemed to have lost the contest. Shuja had reached up to the finals stage twice in such *mohavara* competitions. When he satirised opposing poets his entire body would be on fire. His heart would flutter and a fresh energy would suffuse his body. While replying to the opposing bard's barbs, metrical units such as *raheel* and *fakr* would fluently flow from his lips, much to his own surprise. He would then be infused with boundless enthusiasm causing him to puff up his chest and strut with pride. The thin screech of the *sager* now reminded him of the *mohavara* competition, and provided him with boundless energy.

He was now filled with immeasurable courage. As he sang his compositions inside the cave, the resultant echoes reminded him of the *mohavara* contest and he began leaping around in abandon.

This did not, however, prevent him from collecting his belongings and the *sager* and, negotiating the rockface, vacating his current location. But, as soon as entered the wide open spaces, he had fallen into a swoon for the very first time in his life.

He took a hit of the "secret medicine" he had carefully packed and sat down to sing a poem to his *sager*. At that instant, he thought he saw someone staring at him from the edge of the pool and looked hard at the apparition.

His childhood friend Ali was smiling at him. He appeared to be totally naked and seemed to be beckoning him. Shuja stood up flustered. Ali stood up too. But he no longer resembled Ali. It was Rajendran!

A shocked Shuja called out, "*Ya Hindi ... .keef iji intha hina* (how did you get here)?" In the blink of an eye, Rajendran vanished. Scared out of his wits, confused as to whether it was Ali or Rajendran, the effect of the "medicine" he had consumed having evaporated, he collected his supplies and the cloth bundle containing the *sager*, and staggered downhill. He decided then and there: he would follow the true path of Islam henceforth. He would renounce violence and follow the teachings of the book. He would give up the bedouin ways of feuding and vendettas, give up all his bad habits and follow the true path.

He walked along reminding himself of the lessons he had learnt at his young age in the *madrasa*. He recalled with pride his father's aspiration to see him grow up to be a religious scholar. As he walked quickly, he began to chant the holy lines he had learnt in his youth asking God to protect him from accursed *jinns* and to erase all thoughts of them from his head.

When, finally tired out, he stopped and took a deep breath, he received another jolt. Not far away, five persons were making their way across the desert with their sheep and camel flocks. When he turned away, fearing they were *jinns*, he could see three others making their way towards him with camels. When he made out that the animals were of the *mujahim* and the *maghatir* varieties, he was reassured that they were indeed humans, and not *jinns*, and ran to meet them. He was determined to act normally with them. Displaying none of his fear of *jinns,* he courageously greeted them saying, "As salam alaikum".

All the men towered over him and possessed impressive physiques. He did not understand a word of what they said in response.

Are these Iraqi or Kuwaiti bedouins? I do not understand their language....only a few of their words are comprehensible....are they bedouins at all? Or, could they be *Hindis* or Bengalis? How did they accept an outsider like me into their fold without question? I have never seen an Arab bedouin group do such a thing ... .with their women too casually striking up a conversation with a stranger in this manner.... I know it is normal for bedouin women living in the desert to herd sheep and camels and drive jeeps, but I have never seen one who would mix and speak so freely with a newcomer like these women do.... No way are they Arabian bedus.....these women do not cover their bodies modestly and, in addition, sing and laugh as well?

Not being able to decipher their spoken language, Shuja was a little confused. He accepted their offer of some honey. Their flock consisted of some twenty-odd camels and fifty or so sheep. The women walked alongside their men, unflagging despite the heat.

Unable to follow anything Shuja was saying, they paused for a while and one of them inserted two fingers into his mouth and emitted a shrill whistle. Two whistle blasts immediately came from somewhere in response. The man gave another long whistle in reply to which a short 'phweet' sound came floating in the wind.

Everyone then sat down. Shortly thereafter another man came up to them. Shuja stood up at his approach and wished him, "Harhab". The man too replied politely and, after shaking hands and exchanging kisses with all the other men and women around, he came up to Shuja and enquired after his health and wellbeing, "*Keef al haal? Asak tayyib?*" Shuja felt reassured that there was at least one person who spoke Arabic he could follow.

The man then went on to provide information that amazed Shuja. Their group did not belong to any Arab nation and have lived for ages in this fashion as nomads; they have never settled down at any one spot or carried out agriculture or trade like some of the other bedouins did; they were constantly on the move; they were not citizens of any country and their language was ancient Arabic……and so on and on.

Staying put at one spot was akin to death. It was cowardice. Cheating the natural order. We have been provided legs for the purpose of walking. If they settled down at one location, it meant that they do not respect the legacy of their free-ranging ancestors. As soon as they became agriculturists, notions about conquering the world and controlling time would enter their consciousness. This would only result in strife, disputes, battles and deaths. They presently live naturally without any of these aspects intruding into their lives. The concept of nationhood is totally alien to them.

He went on and on. Shuja too was eager to learn more about their background.

"Are you descended from Adnan or Al Gehthan? Which is your original bedouin lineage?" he enquired.

In response to this query, the tribesman, who was conversing with Shuja in intelligible Arabic, spread his palms wide and admitted, "*Maa adhri* (I don't know)" and added that perhaps his grandfather might know the answer to the question.

When Shuja enquired about his grandfather's whereabouts, he laughed and replied, "*Beit*". These nomads have a home? Maybe the aged among them stay back at a permanent spot, thought Shuja. But, as soon as the thought struck him the man let out another laugh and clarified, "Oh, *beit* means house in your language, doesn't it? In ours, it refers to death….. What you call *qabr* or grave represents 'house' in our speech …." Every word he uttered was pushing Shuja to greater and greater heights of astonishment. He began thinking.

On the one side, there was this human desire for freedom. On the other, the quest for subjugation….. Was this the timeless conflict between humans? Is the world divided by a conflict between order and chaos? In these ultra-modern days of twitter and instagram, how do we even begin to understand a group that does not know, or even wish to learn, about any such devices? As a bedouin myself, even I fail to understand their attitude. How do you evaluate a group that considers an established, stable life contrary to human nature? But, equally, our ancestors must have lived exactly like these people..... did violence and vendetta take root when the bedouins decided to settle down? When an orderly system comes into effect, does violence follow? Are identities such as nation, religion and race the offshoots of violence? Or, is violence an inborn human trait? But then, these people are also carrying firearms?

Do they prefer to spend all their time here because the desert does not impose any restrictions on their lifestyle? The desert, which constantly changes from minute to minute, is indeed a wondrous world. Refusing to conform to human limitations it contains within itself an embryo of constant shift. On the opposite side of the spectrum to its ever-present metamorphosis are the man-made cities, countries and nations.... does everything commence with the family? Family itself is only an arrangement. The focal point for curbing human independence commences with the family....does it mean violence originates from within the family? But, even amongst these people, who wander the desert freely, there is an institution called the family. Or is nature itself a predetermined arrangement? Does the desert, with its so-called perceived freedom, also embody certain restrictions? Aren't water, air, land, sky, stars, moon and sun themselves all part of nature's structure? What about the changing seasons that are consistent? Isn't that an orderly arrangement too? Does nature occasionally shatter its own routine to bloom once again? Are events like the whirlwind, earthquake, drought and flooding revolutionary expressions wrecking nature's structured organisation? Or were they wars waged by elements, invisible to human eyes, like *jinns* for example, against us mortals? Could it be possible that they somehow bring nature under control? Or is it ordained by God? Whatever it is, the desert is the best place on earth for man to live independently. That is because, like the unfettered desert, a man's soul also seeks independence like the unbridled wind. The external world of a man also possesses the same quality of changing every moment of the day, just like the desert….

Shuja walked along mulling over these thoughts. As the sun reached its zenith, they stopped, chanted something and touched the sand to their foreheads. These gestures made him laugh and he wanted to tell them that this was not the right way to offer prayers and that he would show them the proper method. But he gave up the idea as soon as it struck him, and decided he would do so when the time was right. He grew extremely angry when he heard the name of the God they invoked during their prayer. Are they worshipping a false god instead of following Islam? Or, are they inadequately versed in the ways of Islam?

Come to that, I am not a very devoted follower of Islam myself. I have forsaken the rules of peace, amity and affection that Islam preaches and taken to hatred, violence and bloodshed. I have forsaken righteousness. I have committed sinful deeds. I need to reform at least from now on. I should give up frolic and "medicine" during my trips abroad. I need to follow the lead of my sister's husband and emulate his conduct. I will pray five times a day, follow the path laid down in the holy book, avoid picking fights and chart a course to heaven. Enough of this ungodly life. Yes, let me first reform these tribals and bring them to the path of true Islam. Let's teach these barbarians what Islam means and how it will better their lives. This ignorant group of bedus have no idea of what a telephone or the internet means. Let me straighten them out first. I'll slowly bring them to the path of the true religion and then ease them into the modern world. It's my duty to educate my kind….

With these thoughts playing in his mind, Shuja intoned the call to prayer and performed the *dhuhr* prayers. At its conclusion, he smiled at the group and told himself once again 'let me slowly bring them to the true path laid down by God and to the ways of the modern world'. They began walking again.

The new arrival looked at Shuja and asked him where he was coming from. When Shuja fumbled for a response, he said, "I know you belong to the al Sodari bedouin *kabeela*. When my people first saw you, they mistook you for a *jinn*. They were scared you had come from the mystical kingdom of *abqer wadi*," and let out a loud laugh.

Wondering internally how he knew that detail about him, Shuja smiled in reply and asked, "Is it true that the *jinns* have a realm of their own? I've heard some imbeciles in my town also say the same." He decided to continue making casual conversation while watching the man carefully.

In reply, the man burst out laughing and said, "Isn't that where you landed from?"

Shuja was once again stunned into silence. Images of a naked Rajendran surrounded by smoke and the terrain with the pool of water entered his head and rendered him speechless with shock. His brain reverberated with various sounds. As his heart raced in panic, he stood still with his eyes shut for a moment and took a deep breath.

When he opened his eyes, there was nobody around. He began running.

There....in the distance....they were crossing a valley and going on their way.

Standing on top of a sand dune, Shuja watched them walking down below. It was a steep valley. His heart leapt with delight when he saw hundreds of al khozama flowers waving their heads in the wind in the distance. It was a lovely sight.

The heady scent of the al khozama flowers, which bloomed as far as the eye could see, captivated his heart and he felt himself floating in midair. He closed his eyes and inhaled the sweet aroma of the place into his soul. What a surprise? Normally al khozama flowers only bloom during the rainy seasons which follow the winters, he thought to himself and opened his eyes. The sight that met his eyes nearly made him faint with surprise once again, but he gathered himself and watched it keenly.

Standing at some distance, he could see the group gathered around a tree resembling the *samar,* and paying obeisance to it. He began running towards them. He could hear them chanting a verse in front of the tree which grated on his ears and sparked lightning in his eyes. The king of the desert, the *sager*, escaped its cloth wrapping and flew screeching up into the sky.

The screeching sound made Shuja pause and look up. He then felt someone standing behind him and turned around sharply. Once he glimpsed the person, his initial shock turned into relief. The man who had been conversing with him a few minutes earlier was standing there.

“Where are you off in such a rush? To see what they are up to, or to ascertain how the al Khozama bloomed before the rains?” he asked, causing confusion in Shuja’s mind once again. ‘How is he able to fathom what I’m thinking?’ he wondered as he turned to have another look at the bedouins. He was astounded to see that some of them now appeared to be human while the others had taken on the shape of trees. Moreover, they appeared to be swinging from the branches and that sight confounded him even further. The very next moment, both the trees and the men disappeared from his view, and only the Khozama flowers were to be seen blanketing the area. As he stood there in confusion, the tree reappeared along with the men around it. He stood there unable to comprehend the happenings. The beauty of the area and the cool wind that was blowing calmed his mind somewhat. He looked down and saw the fertile soil. He marvelled at the sight of loam stuck to his shoes. He lifted his head and glanced at them once again.

Was that the group of bedus? Or were they mysteries? Were they men or trees? Or, were they switching between men and trees every minute?

The man laughed out loud and addressed Shuja, "The Khozama always blooms here. On days when there are no rains, they bring water from the small dam that you see in the distance over there and pour it over the tree. The very next day, the water stagnates on the ground. That is why the land is always wet and fertile. Are you wondering about a dam in the desert? It was built by the relatives of your great-great-grandfather to store rainwater, which would otherwise go to waste, in the midst of these mountains. And what was your second doubt? Oh, whether they were men or trees, right? They are neither - they are tree-men, true Daseins....tree-men who are the complete antithesis to Martin Heidegger's theory.... Hahaha...." As a blank Shuja ventured tentatively, "I do not understand a word of what you're saying. Excuse me, but I don't recall asking you anything....," he laughed once again and said, "Didn't you ask me just now whether they were men or trees?". He let out another laugh and gestured to Shuja to follow him and both of them began walking towards the bedus. A hundred questions hammered inside Shuja's head: Who is this man? He's talking incomprehensible stuff..... Mentioning names I have never heard before....?

"You're wondering who this Martin Heidegger is, right?" This question shook Shuja up. He stared at him in surprise while the man continued with his tale. He related how a European poet had spent several years living with them in the desert and how both sides had benefited from the interaction, learning from each other. Apparently that man's grandfather had run off to the Arabian desert to escape punishment from Queen Victoria's courts, stayed there until the beginning of World War I and thereafter returned home. Having been fascinated by the tales of the desert told by his grandfather, his grandson had travelled here. He was disillusioned by what he observed, since times had changed, and was about to return home when someone told him about the bedouins still living in the desert. He had immediately set out in search of them. Having immersed himself totally in their ways of life and their poetry, he had finally dropped dead in the desert itself, unable to come to terms with its secrets.

After relating this tale, the man looked Shuja in the face and began to recite a poem:

"Come, my friend,
This is where
Our ancestors lived with their poetry.
They discerned life even in hairs' breadths.
There you can see our epics blooming in the form of Khozama flowers
Look closely my friend, look into my eyes!
Your concern is whether they are men or trees, right?
Do you think the confusion arises because you are observing them from afar?
They would present the same sight even if you were to view them from up close.
That's because it's their true nature with no embellishment.
The same is inside you as well;
It's known as the essence of the desert.
Nothing from the outside world - be it religions, governments,
Wars and battles
Or scientific inventions
Can even touch this landscape.
Moral values that have evolved from
Philosophies derived from personal knowledge or experience,
And greatly cherished elsewhere even today,
Cannot approach anywhere near the desert's pristine nature.
Not just that, even Nietzsche's "Rhetoric" and
Baudrillard's simulacra have to concede defeat before it.
That's the greatness of this desert.
The story of these men, constantly on the move as trees,

Is your own personal story as well.
But,
Caught in the whirlpool of an artificial life,
You stand here
Having lost this wonderful faculty.
If you wish to reconnect with your roots,
You need to plant the desert in your soul.
It will bloom as Khozama flowers and turn into a mighty tree,
And move this earth.
A new classification would then emerge….
Tell me, my friend,
Will you sing about that new genre of nature?
Or, will you revitalise my own personal song?
Your name, your grandfather and great-grandfather's names are all
Nature's realities…..
Sager, Fahad, Shuja…..
Tell me, my friend,
Will you continue my nature's epic from where I left off?

Shuja, unsure how to reply to this *qasida*, responded, "I do not understand everything you say…. But I agree with you on one matter: the desert is indeed a secret treasure trove. But, my friend, I am totally clueless about the other matters you refer to. Were they perhaps the observations of that European poet?" He looked at the man waiting for a reply, hoping to discern his antecedents from the answer.

The man merely smiled and replied, "No … .it was composed by the person who sang about you," and planted another riddle in Shuja's mind.

"The person who sang about me? Who's that? You?"

When he laughed and responded, "Hahaha…..it's actually the listeners," Shuja queried, "Who're they?" hoping to catch a clue from the depth of his voice.

He laughed again and said, "I'll tell you ... .but I'm beginning to have the same doubt as them." Shuja peered into his eyes and asked, "What doubt?" and bristled in anticipation of the hunt.

"Whether you're in reality Shuja or a *jinn*," he replied and grinned broadly. As Shuja was thinking, 'but I never told him my name..... how did he know it?' the man went on, "Your name is Shuja, isn't it? Be that as it may, I told you the listeners were the ones who would write your life's story, didn't I? Do you know who they are? They are the ones who are destined to kill you," he cut the conversation short and prepared to flee the spot.

"What? What did you say? Who are you?" Shuja pounced upon him. Certain that the man was an al Mulaqim who knew all about him, he tried to grab hold of him.

The man easily evaded Shuja's clutches and began running, saying loudly, "Come along, come with me.....let's first ascertain whether these are actually men or trees..... We can sort out our dispute later..... come along.... They'll decide whether you're really Shuja or a *jinn* in human form...." As he raced into the desert, Shuja ran after him determined to catch hold of him.

A thought suddenly struck Shuja and halted his headlong run.

"Who's he? A man or a *jinn*? How did he suddenly make an appearance without a trace? Could he be a *jinn*?

Not sure of the answer to this query, Shuja recommenced his chase.

He felt himself sinking into a pit of quicksand.

***